# PRAISE FOR
# INTO DARK CORRIDORS

*Connie's story is so personal, funny, heartbreaking, and honest. It was incredibly hard to put down because I wanted to know what happened next! Having grown up in a family of home builders, I am very familiar with the process, saw the photos, and visited the home myself but the twists and turns of her story are astounding. This is not just another tale of restoring an old house, it is the story of passion, desperation, dedication, love, and a bit of insanity.*

    — Escott O. Norton, Preservationist,
     historic theatre and home design
     consultant

*Some people are just driven by a vision and that's what historic restoration is all about: the ability to recognize good design and what can be accomplished.*

    — David Lawrence Gray, FAIA

*The author beautifully captures that moment when your head tells you that you are about to jump off a cliff with this enormous project and yet, the heart tells you that you must leap. Coming from a family that has been involved in historic restoration for several decades, I understand that magical pull. What seems utterly crazy becomes a quest that must be completed.*

    — Karen Gray, Associate

*The author's experience with saving a house becomes a practical issue of details – falling in love with the work of artisans from the past. A fascinating account of planning and engineering the move of a 4200 sq. foot structure up a Los Angeles hillside, complete with mishaps and fortunate events.*

— Paul Himmelstein, Fellow and Past President, American Institute for Conservation of Historic and Artistic Works

*The reader laughs out loud, then gasps at the absurd circumstances of a woman who decides to move a huge home through a canyon and restore it, sans husband and sans buckets of cash. Her story covers a vast amount of territory— disassembling and restoring both a home and a young family.*

— Ross Olney, Author

*You can smell the sawdust. With the help of elderly local craftsmen, Connie Hood set out to save an urban treasure. An unlikely cast of local characters and the engineering feat of moving a huge Craftsman home proved to be a surreal and madcap restoration adventure for the entire community.*

— Eric H. Warren, Curator and Past President, Eagle Rock Valley Historical Society, Warner Bros. set designer (ret.)

*A Los Angeles treasure comes to life in Connie Hood's tale of resilience. Elderly neighbors and city archivists help her unravel the story of her old house. History winds backward through 1950s Hollywood, and to the emergence of Los Angeles in 1909. Photos, diagrams, and her account of the restoration journey share a unique experience with the reader.*

— Beth Wladis, VP of Operations, Wade Artist Management, Chief Librarian (ret.) Mid-Manhattan Library, The New York Public Library

*Take a grand old house sliding down into ruin and restore it to glory. Sometimes the client shows up who has no idea what she is getting herself into. Planning these projects takes a lot more time, money and effort than most people realize. When Connie turned to me, I saw challenges and an opportunity. Here was a chance to save a Craftsman masterpiece. With imagination, intelligence and lots of determined follow-through our temporary eyesore on a Los Angeles hillside became a wonderful home full of space, style and beauty unique to the neighborhood"*

— Geoff Sheldon, Architect, LEED AP

INTO DARK CORRIDORS

# INTO DARK CORRIDORS

A Tale of Hands, Heart, and Home

CONSTANCE HOOD

INTO DARK CORRIDORS by Constance Hood

First Edition

Copyright © 2021 by Constance Hood

Published by Waves Press
Ventura, California

www.constancehood.com

Cover design by Jana Rade, Impact Studios Online

Editor: Toni Lopopolo

Library of Congress Control Number: 2021906469

ISBN:   978-09993946-3-2 Paperback edition
        978-09993946-4-9 Digital edition
        978-09993946-5-6 Audiobook edition

Printed in the United States of America

10 9 8 7 6 5 4 3 2 1

xx-v13

*For Eric William Redifer Hood*
*1982-2002*

Betsy –
We need a bigger
hammer!

Connie Hood

# TABLE OF CONTENTS

# FOREWORD

Most house renovations don't involve facing down two rival LA street gangs; battling corrupt bureaucrats; surviving divorce, unemployment, earthquakes, let alone ghosts and a family of owls.

Laugh if you want, but there is a kind of craziness that overcomes people who fall in love with an old house and decide to give up comfort, financial security and the respect of their friends and family to restore the house to some semblance of its former glory. The grander the house and the more decrepit its condition, the greater the attraction—and the insanity.

You may find Connie's story of rescuing Owl's Nest to be funny, incredible, frustrating, enlightening, but by the end you can't help but find it inspiring. Once the old house in the canyon found her, it insisted she breathe new life into the scarred timbers. She listened to its voices. Over the months, the house began to attract the very people that were needed to make living worthwhile.

Few of us would dare take on such an overwhelming project. I should know. I've been a preservation architect for forty years and have watched many a project succeed or fail. Most that succeed have owners with deep pockets or organizations with ample resources. Many that fail have been undertaken by individuals who get in way over their heads because they lack the money or the knowledge of how to proceed. Connie fell in the latter group, but she did not fail.

Why? As she is slowly revealed in her narrative, you come to see the qualities that allowed her to survive this endeavor and thrive. Intelligence, yes, but enhanced by a creativity that allowed her to see through disasters to solutions. Attractiveness, not just to the men who came into her life, but to all the other people who recognized something special in this woman and her project. Perseverance, even when things could not look more hopeless and she didn't know where to turn. Willingness to let others bring their talents and abilities, in whatever quantity, to the project so she did not have to do all the work herself. She credits this special trait to her grandfather, who used his kids and grandkids to renovate houses in her hometown. Of all her qualities, this is probably the most important one she possesses.

Lots of people renovate and even restore old houses. Magazines have been full of their stories for decades. This tale of rescuing what might have become only a pile of scrap lumber and turning it into a grand, warm and loving home is special. The restoration wasn't perfect. The people who effected it weren't perfect. But the results have made for a perfectly delightful book that will warm the hearts of readers, no matter what their houses look like.

Andrea Rebeck, RA
Historical Architect, National Parks Service,
retired

# ACKNOWLEDGEMENTS

This book is a tribute to all the people who helped make it possible to bring an old house out of a canyon and give it a second life. The story is true, parts of it well known to the public and parts deeply personal.

Moving a massive Craftsman home up a Los Angeles hillside became a community project, with support from friends, family, neighbors. Heroes in the adventure include a mortgage banker who helped me find money, a Los Angeles senior inspector who showed us a path through a debris field into a working home and several elderly craftsmen who helped us tackle complex problems. Our friend Stan Lisiewicz dragged his teenaged kids out in a December deluge to construct a working drainage system. Then there is Eric Warren, an Art Director who pushed me forward when I was about to give up. His quick thinking brought in paying location shoots and revived a failing effort. The house became a movie star. A dreamy actor stole my heart and became my husband of 33 years.

Actual writing of the story began as a request from Andrea Rebeck, RA (Foreword). Friends since the age of seven, we were once little girls going around town on bicycles, drawing pictures of grand old houses. She stood by my side as crews cut the house in half and hauled the pieces uphill. After I began writing, I met Toni Lopopolo, agent and editor, who dragged me kicking and screaming through the personal upheaval of a 1980s mother with a big career and a small child, a failed marriage and a hundred tons of scrap lumber.

Former students and neighborhood teens took time to share their stories and interview grandparents about life as immigrant day laborers. Thanks to Eddie Leonardo Perez-Reyes we were able to rebuild authentic scenes with the Central American workers who helped us for months. I'm indebted to several Ventura writers and Beta readers from New York and Los Angeles who asked hard questions and offered feedback on the story while it was in progress.

All of this offered an adventure like no other, the ride of a lifetime.

# PROLOGUE
## SPRING 1986

Two policemen crawled through the opening, following her. Flashlights lit a thirty-year collection of cobwebs, some gray and matted, others silky white with fresh prey folded into delicate netting. To the side, desiccated remains, soft white fur sticking up in patches on leathery hide. No face to identify the animal—probably a coyote kill from a couple years ago. Cat? Rabbit?

"This is kind of creepy." The officer adjusted his gun belt.

Her unspoken words, *oh great—a couple cops afraid of this old cellar?*

"Stairs." Connie pointed, "Just over here—it'll be OK. Watch your heads, there's a bunch of beams."

Connie's got direct lines for both the local fire chief and the police. I'm Owl's Nest, an old house that's seen better days—fires in the hearth and light through my leaded windows, children dancing across thresholds into adult parties. My last owner died here, and I've been abandoned for some years—who knows how many? I can feel all of this in my dried-out siding, once fresh cedar shingles. Dust lies on my windowpanes, at least what's left of them. There's crust on my counters and cabinets, rusted-out toilets and sinks with no faucets. Teenagers break my doors and windows for nighttime parties and spray paint plakas on my lath and plaster walls, defecate on the carpet.

Connie, this thirty-six-year-old mother, has decided that I am worth saving. We have no idea how to make it happen.

# PART ONE

*I would rather be able to appreciate things I cannot have*
*than to have things I am not able to appreciate.*

*Elbert Hubbard*

# CHAPTER ONE

# INTO DARK CORRIDORS WANDERING

## LABOR DAY 1985

Our dream began with a migraine, a stab through the left eye, twirling flashes, and pain pulsing to my crown. The screw then reversed itself and jammed down behind the ear and into my neck.

Friday night I negotiated the freeway until I arrived at the front door of our little bungalow. A carton of Ben and Jerry's Fudge Brownie whooshed through the air. Don called out, "She's home. Run boy! Run!"

Instead of dashing toward his father, two-year-old Eric careened through the room, and stopped at my briefcase, looked up and threw his arms around my legs. Don, Eric, and I flopped onto the brown plush couch and dissolved into laughter, ribbons of chocolate goo and sticky fingerprints marking the stereo speakers and coffee table. In the fridge, probably we'd find a couple raw carrots and maybe wine for Don, a can of cheese ravioli for the boy.

Three days later I still lay on the couch, drained, unable even to whimper into a pillow.

Labor Day 1985, a brutal mix of heat and smog. Brown and yellow weeds filled the canyon behind our bungalow. Dust blew up into the windows along with a lot of noise—chainsaws, laborers in orange suits. At midday, Eric in his Superman pajamas tried to fly by leaping off our dining room chairs. The roaring trucks and guys from the Los Angeles Fire Department brush clearance units had captured his imagination. Don grabbed the red nylon harness, leashed Superman up, and strode off down a grassy path, Eric trotting behind. Heavy equipment buzzed in the canyon below.

The big house in the canyon was a curiosity. We had often set sprinklers facing that parcel, afraid of the canyon fires that storm through Southern California. When Don approached the structure, he found it abandoned. No one lived there. The caretaker's house showed evidence of someone living on site until 1982. Daddy and little boy wandered through the big house, headed back up the hill, and found me on the couch, "Connie, this is something you ought to see."

The migraine hangover droned on. Daylight in our sunny living room made me dizzy and hiking wasn't going to happen.

"Hon, I went through that old house. It's really beautiful, with a lot of interesting woodwork. Please come down with me." I located my darkest black sunglasses and a wet bandanna, and followed him down the path, our toddler in tow. In retrospect, I didn't even know the magnitude of that headache.

The old white house had stood abandoned for years. Paint crumbled over cedar shingles and a black oily discharge leaked through. Sliding glass doors, long since broken out of their bent tracks, served as the entrance to the house. An old pergola stood erect over slabs of broken concrete and faced a side door that led to an empty room with filthy linoleum and Formica counters. We could see wood counters underneath those.

Dark cool rooms pulled me in, a relief from the glaring sun and heat. Who knows how long since someone had lived here? The smell and feel of wood protected us from canyon dust and grit. Unusual entry doors measured fifty-three inches in width, made of heavy quarter-sawn oak that led into the widest hallways I'd ever seen. At some time she welcomed visitors, many of them.

Dirt coated her hardwood floors, some of it loose, some ground in. A living room carpet prompted immediate needs for handkerchiefs, not tissue. I pulled off my bandanna, continuing to step into rooms, and touch her wood. Huge fireplaces had built-in inglenooks. Walked into a library, room after room with cabinetry and closets, porches and balconies. A lovely, vaulted dining room, original tiles. She whispered a vision of soft light and wood polish.

We stepped into the kitchen. Pink and white wallpaper hung in strips. An empty room behind the kitchen showed more broken windows, wood frames pulled off the hinges. Lovely. Spotted burn marks in the floor and the remains of plastic dry-cleaning bags hung from rusty hangers, wrapped around empty light fixtures. All this vandalism—sprayed plakas—gang insignia, shattered windows and caked-up filth. Los Avenues, Cypress Park and others had laid claim to the old house.

"My God Don, she's a mess, but we used to clean up really funky messes in Grandpa's apartment houses. Someone can paint over spray paint; repair these plaster cracks. Dammit, I wish they weren't breaking the windows. That's a lot of work." It was evident that a wealthy person with some taste should undertake a restoration of the home.

Who built this once beautiful house, who abandoned it and why?

# CHAPTER TWO

# GHOSTS

"**D**on found a house!"

Silence, then a response. "That's nice dear."

I juggled the phone in one hand, a peanut butter sandwich in the other, hungry child nipping at it.

"No, Mom, I mean, Don and I went to that old white house in the canyon. That place, it's really interesting, but no one's been there for years."

Mom laughed. Our family had bonded over tools and buckets of paint, long work days in hot sun or in frigid rooms, repairing decrepit Victorians in Elmira, New York.

"No, like our Victorians, but really old. Not sure what you'd call the style. You could roller skate in these rooms—kind of like the Tudor palaces in England, but not lords and ladies, it's kind of plain." A pause, mom's thoughts whirring in the background. She's the art teacher.

"Or at least it would be plain, but some of it is like Uncle Dean's wood puzzles, impossible joints, kind of fancy wood. If it were polished, but it's all dirty. No one's been in there for years."

"There's a bunch of beams downstairs, massive posts, and lots of overhangs, but not slipshod. Looks more like outside shelter. Porches everywhere, even in the bedrooms."

"Anyway, they pulled all the brush away from it, and..."

I'm not sure why I made that phone call about an abandoned

house in the canyon. We hadn't found anything. The house had sat there all the time.

Our little bungalow perched at the top of the hill. Don and I made our expenses every two weeks, spent all our money shortly after each payday. When I hired a cleaning lady to mop up the house after my sixty hour workweeks, Don commented, "My family didn't have servants, they *were* the servants." He loved to talk about his parents' hardscrabble home in Crab Orchard, Kentucky, which he'd never visited.

Don, Eric and I hiked down the hill to visit our find. Our boots skidded on the dusty slope, dry after the blazing summer months.

"Con, watch out for those gopher holes. Snakes live in them."

I lifted Eric over landmines of gopher holes, watched out for coyote scat.

Following Don, I stepped across the broken concrete and smashed glass of the patio, over a broken aluminum threshold leading into the dark rooms.

Old house smell, that smell of dust and age. Exactly what is this? Remains of illness and death from people who overstayed? Illness leaves a cloying sour smell, age leaves complex layers from lives that have been lived. A feral cat scurried through the living room, yellow eyes and mottled dark fur never brushed, her belly sagged from endless litters. I found part of the smell—that mama cat marked every inch of the downstairs. A crusted carpet of no color covered the living room to the blackened fireplace. Broken windowpanes, bashed-in glass doors provided plenty of ventilation, but a fit of sneezing dammed up my throat.

I'm from upstate New York. My family lived in old houses. Not sure if that's what they liked, or the fact that old Victorians came cheap. In the 1950s, Grandpa and Uncle Bill bought and restored nine hometown Victorians slated for tear down. Each house divided into four seniors' apartments for people who couldn't take care of a big home anymore.

In 1961 Grandfather Westervelt bought a house for Mom, my brother and me. Mom, the Beatnik art teacher, thrilled to finally have her own place. When most everybody in town tore down Victorians to put up cubes of aluminum siding, Mother worked on her blue and purple vision. On school day afternoons, we hurried home and suited up for evenings of scraping, painting, and mixing wallpaper glue. Dressed in our uncle's old shirts and bandannas, work continued until bedtime. The bandannas picked up sweat on necks, kept paint and glue from getting into hair and eyes. All of us suffered with allergies, but our bandanas filtered out coal dust and animal dander. The family looked like a gang of outlaws.

Westervelts are born with sawdust in their veins. Each child had a specialty. I painted elaborate woodwork, colored fish scales, window sashes and porch spindles. Received an elegant paintbrush for my tenth birthday, genuine sable hair, angled to keep paint drops out of tight corners. Older kids learned to remove peeled paint with sharp scrapers, and to call an adult if they found dry rot. Even the littlest kids had jobs. Somewhere around your fourth summer you got your sand block. Toddlers learned to roll putty worms. I supervised the little ones between licks with my new sash brush.

Back in the present, a dream seen a hundred times before. I saw this grand parlor with polished wood and fresh paint, an imaginary dining room chandelier. Upstairs rooms of this big house didn't collect as much filth as the entry rooms. A sweet, neglected bedroom had two dormers, and its peeling pink wallpaper let me know the room once housed little girls, cozy and safe with their secrets. Two large walk-in closets had poles for hanging dresses, wide shelves ready for stacked hatboxes. Don and Eric poked around the boys' room, closets, sleeping porches, Don's flashlight prying here and there at cobwebs and old secrets.

That evening we trailed back to our bungalow and I phoned Uncle Bill. No one else knew old buildings like my house-whisperer uncle. I learned craftsmanship under his guidance. Wondered what he'd think about this curious development in our neighborhood. No decision to make, but it would be tragic if vandals or a canyon fire destroyed the old house. Uncle Bill's full plate included teaching and getting his affairs in order. His doctors finally diagnosed the unknown virus, a new disease called AIDs. The day he told me he would die, I couldn't understand him. My grandparents had died, but Uncle Bill's illness fell into uncharted territory. What did he face? I felt lost in the darkness along with him, no road map for a life without him.

Uncle Bill and a friend drove to Los Angeles. Gaunt and beard-ed, his brilliant blue eyes flashed with curiosity. He and his friend walked down the hill, taking time to breathe and rest. I had no idea how we were going to get him back up. All of us stopped in the big downstairs dining room to catch our breaths. Uncle Bill ran his hands along the tall window casements. He studied a broken light fixture hanging by a single wire.

"I think this was built around 1910. What a spectacular ex-ample of California architecture." His practiced eye followed the vaulted ceiling, an unusual feature in a Craftsman home.

"Con, this is worth about four times as much as the house you live in, and it'll cost you that much again to fix it up." He walked around the vast empty room. "You're going to need cash and antiques."

Uncle Bill studied the graffiti in the hall, then looked toward the city streets that ran up to the gates of the old ranch. "What's in the streets over there? What kind of homes?"

Don and I knew both answers: a rough neighborhood inhabited by gangs and drug dealers.

"People say this old ranch is owned by a developer. There's a huge fight about someone who wanted to put in low cost apartment blocks here, like 400 units."

"You know, Con, you might need to move this, especially if a real estate developer owns the canyon. Look at all this vandalism. The gangs will burn this place down some day."

Our fantasy halted at "move the house."

Uncle Bill's dreams had finished as well. AIDS transformed elegant features into gray crags and shadows. Courage and mortality in the final struggle, beaten by disease, death's veil descending over him.

The puzzle of the old landmark began to reveal itself. The previous owner, a Hollywood manager, had left years before when age and illness caught up with him. His old caretaker remained on the ranch until death took him as well. Lifelong residents of the neighborhood came by and told of hiking down here in their childhood to pet animals, see Western movie stars ride their horses in the canyon. Nowhere near Hollywood, the ranch was a place to host Hollywood parties, just people and horses. In a flash I understood why more than 100 empty gallon wine bottles lay in the cellar. Those earned a decent burial.

A simple cleanup wouldn't make things right. Rusted farm equipment lay around the rundown outbuildings, old iron too large and too heavy to haul away. Maybe I could find the owners or heirs to the house. The old house spoke to me in torrents of language I didn't understand. How do you find a millionaire?

A friend suggested Heritage Square, an outdoor museum of

historic Los Angeles homes situated next to the Pasadena Freeway. The park marks the entrance to Mt. Washington and we had never visited. On Sundays, docents in period clothing led visitors through the houses. With Eric in tow, Don and I entered the park.

"How did you move these buildings here?"

The docent said, "Becomes a real challenge. They don't look anything like this when Cultural Heritage brings them here." She adjusted the ruffled apron over her long skirt. "Let's go see the one on the end. That one moved here, let see, been about six months."

Scaffolding covered high walls of bare wood grayed with age. Workers laid slate tiles on the roof, to seal it before the winter rains.

At the site, the docent said, "This came over in three pieces, and we've reassembled it on site."

Don told her about the house in the canyon. "So, anyway, what would a historian recommend?"

"Oh, they come out really nice when you do the work."

Don and I entered a colorful Victorian and stood in a shiny foyer from more than a century ago. Time had simply disappeared.

The docent said, "You know, there's a gorgeous move-on in Pasadena. I'll give you the name and number of the man who's restoring that beauty."

We bit. What damage could one more house tour do? Maybe that millionaire would have a millionaire friend who would fall in love with "our" house.

The Pasadena house resembled grand Victorians I'd grown up with in Elmira, pristine white work, leaded glass, hydrangea bushes. I felt homesick for a town I hadn't lived in for twenty years, for large families, children playing, women sipping tea and men in deep conversations.

The Pasadena owner took pride in his work. "What you need

to do is call Valley House Movers. This house came over in two pieces, and I've been working on it about eighteen months."

A house move, far beyond our means and abilities, but how could it possibly hurt to learn more about the process? I wrote down the number of the house mover and jammed the scrap of paper in my purse.

After lunch, we wandered into the canyon again. All three of us, Don, me, Eric, fascinated by the untold story of this house. Someone had loved this old house to their dying breath.

The nursery faced into the canyon, banks of windows, tin lined toy chests, and a fireplace. I lifted a chip of paint with my fingernail, not the sticky acrylic that we use now, but layers of oil, spread thin over lath and plaster. The chip broke into flakes, the flakes crumbled. Picked off another chip. No microscope, no chemical analysis, no color analysis. I poked away at the plaster, surprisingly strong, but already marred with spray paint messages from the gangs.

Eric played on his blanket. This afternoon he lugged his largest toy down the hill, a huge Lego ferryboat that held cranes, cars, little trucks, little men. He examined the ship, and pulled off all the trucks, lined them up.

"Men work! I work the men!"

He pulled off the wheelhouse, and its little captain took a place at the head of the trucks. "You men work! Open hole." The little boss gave commands to unload and reload the hold, lift the little bricks with the crane. Eric used a piece of twine to drag his boat around the room.

He spent the entire afternoon taking his loading equipment apart and putting it back together again.

# CHAPTER THREE

# WHOSE WAS THIS?

The new owners of my company presented a motivational seminar. "We kill our wounded and we eat our dead."

The 1980s workplaces were all about mergers and acquisitions, a corporate version of PACMAN, and some people were getting rich. The rest of us bounced around game boards as moving figures —a relocation here, a reassignment there. I lost my job. Don and I needed to find someone with a lot of cash and expertise to save the old house.

The upside? Severance pay and time to pursue a quest. The first task involved waiting in lines at the Los Angeles Hall of Administration. Who pays property taxes on the canyon? The printout stated that the old house and thirty-five acres belonged to DDW Associates in Costa Mesa. Time for a sales call. Put on a business suit and locate the hair spray. Find out what is at 3200 Bristol in Costa Mesa.

I ended up at Downey Savings, a multi-story bank. Lobby screens did not indicate the name of DDW Associates, so I strolled to a desk and asked to meet with the president of the bank. Maybe I'd at least get a real estate VP to talk. The lady ushered me upstairs.

Mr. D. introduced himself, president of Downey Savings.

"Thank you for meeting me, sir. I live on Mt. Washington, and I'm looking for DDW Associates. They own the land next to my home. A wonderful old house sits there, and it's being vandalized."

He leaned back in his chair and looked around the room while I described the house. "A fabulous piece of architecture. Early 20th century—massive wood beams, broad porches, everything hand hewn."

"How interesting." Mr. D. sat forward and looked me in the eye.

"I've never heard of it. I don't think we have any holdings in LA."

He paused. "Where exactly is Mt. Washington?"

The long day and a tank of gas got me nowhere.

Don and I stepped into a hot mess. Neighbors got involved, not too happy about our probe. DDW had plans to install hundreds of high-density condominiums on the thirty-five-acre ranch. Their "affordable units" were being bitterly fought by people who had invested in homes on top of the hill, overlooking the canyons. At the association meeting, people argued about everything from street repairs to coyote habitats. Neighbors wanted walking trails and open views for their homes, but no one planned to ante up any cash to buy the land. They all agreed to block the development permits, and who the hell wanted that big old house? What an eyesore.

One neighbor pushed me forward into the quest. "You might find something at the Gamble House in Pasadena. They have an architecture library."

The library volunteer listened to my tale. "I found a house—it looks a lot like this, but it's all run down." I displayed a packet of photographs and began to fan them out on the counter.

"There's these big rooms, the beams, and a huge fireplace. Really complicated woodwork, but not carved." The librarian looked at the dark images, empty rooms, torn drapes, but just enough sunlight streaming through to illuminate the woodwork.

"Would you like to look at some books on Craftsman architecture and see if you can find something similar?"

Craftsman. That word again. The archive photos showed wide porches and comfortable rooms that ushered in the 20th century. I read on. Natural materials, handmade details and no ornament without a utility.

Two-year-old Eric sat down on the library rug. As long as the crackers and puzzles held out, he managed his behavior in libraries and old houses. The curator came by, and we began to discuss the house. To my surprise Eric actually paid attention to adult conversations. A tiny voice piped up. "Somebody ruin my scary house, and I have to clean it all up." What made him think that? Scary? I should have worried, but not that afternoon.

I poured through more books and periodicals about turn of the century houses. Just one more page turn, and there I saw it, an inglenook and tapestry brick fireplace, very similar to the one in the old house. Built by Louis Easton. I scribbled the name "Louis Easton" in my notebook. The cover of the book caught my attention. Author, Dr. Robert Winter, a professor from my alma mater. I picked up a sleeping toddler. Next stop: run home to use the telephone.

Nobody graduated Occidental College without Dr. Winter's humanities courses and lectures on architecture. The Alumni Office listened to my story of the old house and gave me a phone number. I phoned Dr. Winter with my tale, and within minutes a brown Volkswagen Rabbit pulled into my driveway. Out jumped a bald smiling man in tennis shoes and a plaid shirt. "Let's see what you have."

We started to walk down into the canyon and he stopped, "Oh my, oh my.... Yes, yes, it has Easton's look all over it."

"Watch out for all this glass."

We stepped inside to the teak lined library. Wooden book-shelves and filing racks still intact.

Dr. Winter poked his fingers along the details—complex join-ery, wood fitted like a puzzle around every corner in the house. "This is by a master builder. Easton basically worked on site, supervising every phase of craftsmanship and design, but he wasn't a registered architect in 1909. We may not be able to locate an architect."

We walked into the kitchen.

"Oh dear, I wish they hadn't damaged that floor. You can't get that lumber anymore."

"Connie, we must save this. The trick will be keeping it safe until we find somebody to take on the restoration. But, let me talk to the city first. I'm going to recommend immediate protective status." Two days later the copy of Bob Winter's letter arrived in the mail. Don and I were invited downtown to a review board meeting.

The white limestone edifice of City Hall rises above a park full of derelicts, the point and beacon representing what was once the tallest building in Los Angeles. A modernist rainbow sculpture, weather-beaten, supposed to bring magic of colored lights and music to the plaza below, hadn't worked in years.

Up the stairs into the maw of the building, catacombs of hall-ways with a dizzying selection of departments, hundreds of them. Don and I strode along the polished concrete halls until we reached a brass nameplate on a door—Cultural Heritage Commission. The letter from Dr. Robert Winter introduced us and our story. "Mr. and Mrs. Redifer? Please, take these two seats on the end, and tell us what you have found."

Commissioners, a blur of gray and beige suits, glasses with thick plastic frames, beards and conservative hairdos, characters from a Frank Capra movie or any black and white picture from the past. Dr. Winter's letter set up more questions than it answered.

"What did we know about the property? The architect?" The city councilmember and the commission could get protective status on the old house while we all sought out the millionaire preservationist.

The commission president studied our photographs and turned to us.

"You got a screwdriver?"

Don and I exchanged confused glances.

"Get in there this afternoon and get those light fixtures out before someone damages them."

I looked at Don. He needed to be back at school for lunch duty. He shook his head.

"I have to go back to work."

"Please call your school and take the afternoon off. This is important. We'll find the owners for you, and you can replace the fixtures at a later date. Right now, you need to secure them."

The light fixtures? There were no crystals, no stained glass, and no shiny metal tubes. I didn't even know they were supposed to be beautiful. Torn paper sockets and everything aged to a filthy dark brown obscured hand constructed brass and copper work. Within an hour Don and I had toolbelts on and were handing hardware to each other. By day's end, we'd packed sixteen crates of light fixtures into our garage. Spaghetti boiled in the pot when our phone rang.

"Mrs. Redifer? This is Camille Courtney, vice president of Downey Savings."

"Why are you making all this mess with the city?" I could feel the anger on the other line. The anger went both ways. I'd driven sixty miles to that bank, where the president stated he knew nothing about any property in Los Angeles.

Suddenly that old house mattered. It was scrap lumber, and a neighborhood nuisance, slated for removal. Ms. Courtney had already shown the plans at association meetings. The entire canyon and its stands of trees and rocks would be bulldozed for the condominiums.

She listened to my protest. "But what will you do about the house?"

"We will raze it the moment permits are issued."

I continued, "That house should be restored, even if someone has to be move it. It's a wonderful example of early California architecture, and the structure is pretty much intact."

"...and what do you propose we do with it?"

"There must be someone who wants it very much. I would do anything to have a place like that."

"That old thing? You can have it. Just get it off our land."

# CHAPTER FOUR

# PRESERVATION COMMANDOS

I looked at Don, drew in a deep breath.

"Hon, what?"

"That was the bank Vice President. She says we have six months to get the old house off their land."

The next morning's phone call went right through to Ms. Courtney.

"Yes, if you want that old house, we'll send you a caretaker appointment along with our Terms and Conditions. You'll have six months to figure out the rest, while we complete our plans for development of the canyon property."

The Special Delivery envelope arrived in a day. What had I done? This house sat beyond our reach in every way: too large, too damaged plus the impossible idea that it had to be moved. Me out of work, with time to fantasize a life as a house pet in some other existence, playing with my toddler and other little kids in the mornings, an interview or three. Enjoy our little bungalow until I could return to work.

True, Don knew how I loved old houses. Old houses framed our dreams, a blending of past fantasies and compatible realities. He'd never lived in a restored house, but now he spent every free afternoon walking through the rooms of *our* old house.

Weekend evenings we kept watch over the place from our kitchen windows. Late on a Friday night, lights flashed in the dark. Don spoke, "Looks like we have visitors." Eight of them, six boys and two girls scrambled through the weeds, got in through the open back patio.

Don changed into all black—jeans, turtleneck, a belt full of all sorts of things I'd never seen before. The last article on the belt? A brand new Motorola radio. He handed me the walkie-talkie, we reviewed our signals. I kept my radio open to listen. The Black Knight strode off. Better him than me. I had to fall asleep every night with the "bang, bang" din of his cop shows.

As soon as he disappeared, I worried, sat in a silent kitchen with a child on a booster seat. Yes, we understood that the big house faced demolition. However, our conversations hadn't extended to the idea of putting ourselves in harm's way.

Stepping into the old house from a side door, Don stopped in a darkened stairwell, listened for disturbances before he shooed the kids out. Heavy steps and a crack of breaking wood announced mischief. Two thugs got up on the inglenook bench; one snapped open a knife.

"Shit man, that's some blade." His pal gouged into pristine teak woodwork, *Cypress Park*, their gangster plaka.

"*Los Avenues* not gonna paint over this!"

"Yeah, and the bitches can't scrub this shit off."

No movement from Don.

Talking and laughter from the kids, a snap of a beer can, crackle of chip bags. Teenagers with eleven-year-old brains. Good God in heaven. Some of those girls hiked through the weeds in high heels, hair and sweaters full of burrs. They sat on beat-up old carpet that reeked of cat piss. A feral cat sauntered through the room, glared at the intruders, disappeared to catch dinner.

Don waited in the hall, quiet, still.

Thank heavens the punks didn't go to the trouble of gathering kindling to set a fire in the fireplace. They came through a canyon full of walnut branches that the fire department left on the ground. Nice wood, hard, burns hot. These kids grew bolder over the past year, claiming territory, fighting at least two other gangs. Didn't want to lose their party house, so, no fires.

They looked up. A tall man stood right in the middle of the living room, red beard, beaked nose, sharp as a hawk's. At least that's what they saw before his 300-candlepower cop flashlight lit up eight faces. Don, aka "Red," disciplinary dean at the largest high school in Los Angeles, had to deal with gang members on a daily basis. The kids, blinded by the light, looked up, confused. Meanwhile, Don's memorizing features. His qualifications for this, in addition to a literature degree? Red grew up in Venice knife fights.

A deep resonant voice: "You're trespassing. You need to leave."

"We just a few friends, we doin' no harm."

Red's hooded eyes didn't blink, an owl on the hunt.

"I won't repeat myself."

"Who the hell are you?"

"I'm the caretaker."

"What? This old house's got no caretaker."

"Actually, she does now. You can listen to me or you can listen to the police. I really don't care."

Don kept a knife holstered in his back pocket, another one sheathed in his boot. In his hand he held a small radio. His voice deep and strong enough to command the situation.

"Shit, we don't want no trouble with cops. This dude's creepy." A lean dark-haired boy in an immaculate white T-shirt spoke first. The entire group dressed in white T-shirts, bleached and pressed. Some of them even pressed their jeans. Expensive athletic shoes, no athletes here.

Don pulled a paper out of his pocket, unfolded it. As legal guardians we had full rights to remove trespassers. Northeast Police and the Battalion Chief for the Fire Department granted us private lines for immediate backup and support. The old house might be a neighborhood nuisance, but now she was our nuisance, official as hell. I listened as Don gave them the bum's rush.

"Hey Mister, can we at least finish our beers?"

"You have one minute."

The boys chugged back the second six-pack.

Don's voice again. "Party's over."

He pressed the button on the radio. Static. That afternoon, we'd come down to test the walkie-talkie radios to make sure the signals worked on the hill.

"Blue? You there?"

"Affirmative, Red."

"We've got visitors. They want to meet Northeast Police."

"Standing by."

He stood over the group. A couple guys still on the floor, others found their feet. The two babes watched from the inglenook.

"Here's the deal. You do as I say, or you do as LAPD says."

"Okay mister, we're going." They head out to the brush then the dirt road that led down toward Division Street. Division near Verdugo, called a no man's land, drag races, nightly gunfire, damn helicopters at all hours.

"And by the way, tell your friends that this house is no longer available to them or anybody. It's getting cold at night anyway; you'd be better off at home. It's Friday night. Why don't you go to a football game or something?"

They scurried off, Don posted himself at the doorway, moved through the house to make sure no other punks hid out, pushed the button on the radio.

"Blue, all clear."

Red hikes back up the hill to a cold beer.

On Sunday morning Don, Eric and I piled into Don's Subaru, drove around the hill and up the dirt road to the front door of the old house. New supplies, fresh from Ole's Hardware Store, jostled in the back—two trashcans, a snow shovel, brooms. We pulled up to the side door. We wrapped three wet bandannas over our faces, I tied Eric's bandanna in back, slipped mittens on the little guy.

"Eric, you can help mommy and daddy!" I showed him how to pick up bottles and cans and take them to the trashcan, fun game for a toddler.

"Don't touch your face with the mittens. You'll get them really dirty." Why did I bring a three-year-old into this mess?

"See the broken glass here? Call mommy when you find that. Never, ever touch the broken glass or anything sparkly. Big owie!"

Don and I, in new leather work gloves, picked up broken glass and fallen plaster. The feral cat wandered in and out, watched, hissed. Don kept a sharp eye on the cat, made sure Eric didn't try to play with the kitty. The kid couldn't resist an animal.

We learned that our treasure actually housed more than one gang, rival gangs to be exact, and they fought constantly. Cypress Park met on the Division Street side of the hill. The territory on the Figueroa Street side belonged to Los Avenues. One gang used black spray paint, the other marked in yellow. Every light-colored wall covered in spray paint. Didn't bother with the black and pink patterned fifties wallpaper. One weekend, black graffiti messages marked the plaster, and days later, yellow *plakas* obscured the graffiti. Eventually, they broke off plaster on the wall between the nursery and the girl's bedroom. Their fists couldn't break through the fireplace bricks or the hard maple bookshelves. The nursery woodwork got a reprieve.

After a second or third visit, it became clear the gangs had no intention of leaving. Near the back door, Don found a lead pipe broken off from old plumbing. He showed it to me.

"You know what this is?"

"A pipe?"

"A lead pipe meant for me. They intend to take me down with this. Con, that's deadly force."

Careful discussion and checking with the bank's legal confirmed the caretaker authority. It matched the rights for our own bungalow up the hill.

Don began carrying the Glock.

# CHAPTER FIVE

# DRIVING IN CIRCLES

My career stalled. I drove Don's Subaru in circles around the city stuck, not in traffic, but in everything else. Baby sound asleep in his car seat. Behind the wheel, at least you move.

After eleven years of premium salary, company car, and free trips, I had nowhere to go. No more guys who phoned after lunchtime martinis to talk about oversold hotels, airlines that flew everywhere, cars that conked out 75 miles from nowhere. Retaining client contracts wasn't even about them. It's about cost controls when you're moving hundreds of people. My closet sat full of designer suits, silk blouses and heels, a drawer full of lipstick smiles.

In fall 1985 grubby jeans stiffened with each meal and cleanup.

The bungalow's back fence faced the canyon, also the gaping wound in the back of the big house. I swear that house spoke to me. Nonsense. What would she say? She's sad. Well, I'm not happy with myself. Her very existence will depend on what we do? The decisions we make? Good luck with that. I'm not to be trusted. She likes my hands. They have touched her wood, thrown out trash, wiped down an unused kitchen.

I turned back to our living room mess. We'd have been better off living in a hamster cage with little notebooks and papers scattered everywhere, to say nothing of too many books. Fluffed pillows on an ugly brown plush sofa. Picked up scraps of paper and an empty vodka bottle off the cluttered coffee table, an old ship's hatch cover coated with resin. Comments and notes about the big house. Don's late-night writing.

Hmm, no harm in putting together a notebook for the big house. A record someone can use to speed up the salvaging or saving. Unanswered questions become the root of problems. I could think them through and organize the bits for somebody. First question, "How do you move a house?"

Unloaded my purse for the scrap of paper with a phone number for Valley House Movers, as well as any spare change that might be hiding at the bottom under the lint.

"What do we need to do?" The house mover came out and described the process. Dave, all business, clean jeans and slicked back hair, ground dirt under fingernails from years of heavy labor.

"Well ma'am, you're gonna need a foundation."

"So, I build a foundation and they set the house on top of it?

"No, we don't come out and set the house on a foundation. A house is full of working systems, pipes that bring in water and heat, electrical, that sort of thing. You don't just guess where all the pipes and mechanicals should go."

I'd never given a thought about what existed under the floors of my house. The nearest I'd come to any of this? A clogged toilet. Effluence had to flow somewhere.

"Um, how does it work then?"

"Well, houses don't fly except in the movies. Can't lift 'em."

Wait, if you can't lift a house, how do you move one?

"What we do is bring the house to the new location and set it up on cribbing, layers and layers of big timbers, kind of like your childhood Lincoln Logs set. The foundation contractor gets underneath and builds the foundation, complete with all the utility hookups. Your foundation pipes get you to the city sewers or your septic system. Then we come back and lower it into the foundation. Do you have an architect yet?"

"Excuse me?" In my mind the architects already planned and built this house eighty years ago.

"You'll need an architect to draw up the foundation plans before we can do anything."

"Who knows an architect, someone who could draw up plans?" Inquiries at neighborhood potlucks led right back to Heritage Square, a guy named Geoff. Nice guy. He schlepped out to Mt. Washington, looked at the house.

"Well, we'd need to draw up a foundation, and I've got the engineering background to set this thing into a hill. You've got to go through City Plan Check. Where will you move the house?"

Good question. Not a clue. I called Downey Savings. Our existing bungalow sat on a corner, the lot a minimal grade, maybe twenty degrees, but someone carved out our lot for the bungalow. The land adjacent to us, the same, fairly level. Would the bank be willing to sell us that piece? Not that I could buy much of anything except oatmeal and milk that month. Didn't hurt to ask, right?

Camille at the bank got back to me. "Yes, that might be possible. The top of the canyon might be set aside for greenbelt, so the big house could go there. How much land do you think you'd need?"

Geoff, the architect, suggested a large double lot. "Let's say a half acre? It's a big house and if DDW develops the canyon, you don't want a bunch of condos at your property line."

Sure, what would that cost? About $60,000? Ka-ching! It's not as if we were doing any feasibility study. How do people finance these things? No one lends money on land, or on structures that are not habitable.

A million other questions turned into little lists and flow charts, not neatly drawn in lines on the pages, but wrapped around corner margins or falling off the edge of the paper. Maybe the mystery millionaire would thank me for my work. In cash.

Geoff again, "Oh, you'll need to hire an engineer and a geologist."

"Why?"

"They need to find out if it's feasible on the land you're looking at."

"What?"

"Examine for earthquake faults, soft soils, expandable stuff like clay that causes mudslides, that sort of thing. Also, if you're able to get the lot in the canyon, we won't try to take it out over a street. You'll need to bulldoze the canyon."

Up to my ears in learning about reports and studies that taxed everything I'd ever learned in geology and physics classes. As a student, "Who needs this stuff? Why would I need to learn all that anyway?"

Luckily, I'd paid just enough attention to start talking through the proposed engineering. At some point, I would get a new job and stop this game. I hadn't yet dealt with City Planning or heaven forbid, the neighborhood council that already labeled that bank a nemesis to our quiet way of life on Mt. Washington. That'd be like swatting a beehive off the eaves with a paintbrush, which I'd seen my grandfather do once. Yikes.

Eric's grandfather Chuck called, his weekly update with Don. Don began chatting about the big house, covering the fact that I was still unemployed and we were broke.

"Say Chuck, have we told you about that old house in the canyon?" I never could grasp the idea that Don sometimes skated —related incomplete information, then let us believe we'd forgotten something.

"Anyway, it's really interesting—lots of old-fashioned wood-work. A bank owns the land, and they've made me caretaker until we can figure out what should be done with the place...."

Chuck bit.

"Why don't I come out on Saturday?"

Don always joked about being bred in an aviary—laid in a hammock with a pile of books and some seeds. Chuck loved birds, but affection for Don showed through in the way he took care of us all. Don's mother died years ago, but some emotions never die. Chuck shrouded himself in grief and planned to join his ghost bride soon, wherever she'd gone. Every day he worked in his garden and on his home, waiting. A loved one can be buried in a grave, but the love remains. His time hadn't yet come, his solitude a burden.

Chuck drove out to take a look-see, blue eyes twinkling above sunburned cheeks. Draping from the ends of his arms were hands that were connected up through the entire body with muscles and sinews. Deep veins told stories of love and war. Chuck could grasp a saw or a pistol with equal precision. Those arms could gently embrace those he held dear or take down an intruder. A gentle smile and a white beard finished the picture. He could be Santa, and he could be formidable.

His calloused hands held a grizzled black poodle. "Can Blackie walk?" The idea of an animal always held in someone's arms fascinated Eric.

Chuck set down the dog, "She'll only pee on real grass." He squinted at the white house below. He picked up the dog and we trudged down the hill to see Don's new obsession.

A retired school custodian, Chuck spent thirty years replacing broken windows, cleaning, repairing, painting. He'd seen vandalism every week. "Don, we could clean this up and paint it—look at all these rooms." A new version of the dream began to appear. Chuck and Don began talking about the four of us living together in the big house one day, live-in day care for Eric, and a new life for desperately lonely Chuck.

Afraid I didn't really pay attention.

Uncle Bill's last request was for a champagne brunch with all of us in his Point Loma home. The master bedroom had a picture window view of the ocean where he'd body surfed daily for more than ten years. Today he lay under blankets, chilled and feverish in his own bed. The mimosas came from fresh oranges and champagne. Uncle Jack, always the host, made sure that platters of food came upstairs.

Our talkative family was quiet, trying to make conversation about a future that would not include Uncle Bill, but maybe shaped by his legacy. The half-knitted sleeves of a sweater lay across my lap, my fingers flying through wool fast enough that no one could see my hands tremble. The thing about imminent death? Everyone's afraid. The central figure may or may not be at peace. How could anyone feel at peace with any of this?

On December 9 the light went out in the midst of black thunderclouds, and a few white gold rays peeking through—a divided sky, a divided soul. The curtain dropped. Uncle Bill's final act ended, we filed out in silence without a sound.

Actually, that's not true. I sobbed all night, drank two glasses of wine, and vomited up everything that I'd put in my body for a week.

Two weeks later Bill's ashes joined his beloved waves forever.

And so we lick our wounds of the heart. We can't lead or guide the person who leaves us. We can only follow, but we don't.

Depression hit, the body slam of a large and powerful wave. The days continued to shorten, I slipped into an endless night–not a clear black night with shiny stars, ways that you could see through to the heavens, but a dark and cloudy night, when the sky becomes the color of charcoal, lit by a moon, but a moon that you can't see —no light, no heat. Just mist, but you can't see how you are going to press forward, or through, or any direction at all.

No way to drive out of this one.

# CHAPTER SIX

# HISTORY REPEATS

I stood in the library with Geoff, our architect. Don and I could not request bids or assemble a budget until we had a general plan of what needed to be done, a timeline, estimated expenses, and ways to leverage funding. Somehow, we scraped together $300 for advice.

Geoff looked around the room with the elaborate teak built-ins. "So, what do you know about this house?"

"Not much. Couldn't find any real history. We traced the developer through City Hall, but the trail stopped there."

I looked around the room, teak shelving wiped clean. Built-ins filled the home, tin-lined cabinets inside benches, bookshelves, cabinetry. No need for standing furniture, or heavy carved Victorian armoires or sideboards. Open floor plans distinguished this modern home of 1909 from Victorian counterparts. Simple wooden posts and beams separated the large downstairs social rooms.

After the cook cleared dinner, a bustling matron in a simple linen dress and knitted shawl might have organized evenings around the fireplace, stories or poems from the bookshelves or perhaps singing around the piano. In contrast to Victorian high society, elegance redefined itself as informal and socially enlightened. No doubt her plain linen dress worked well with a broad brimmed hat and a Suffragist sash. In this large open space, a woman expressed her opinions in mixed company. In this modern home, no doors separated the men's port and cigars from women's gossip and card games.

Daydream over. I returned to 1985.

"Geoff, I've never confirmed the original architect—whoever designed all this. Dr. Winter at Occidental College wrote the letters to the city. The inglenook, fireplace and built-ins match the work of Louis Easton from Roycroft. Dr. Winter's books have photos that look a lot like this, but we don't have signatures on documents."

"No, what I mean is, who lived here?"

"Any ideas how to go about finding out?"

"Go down to the County Hall of Records. You should be able to find handwritten books and parcel maps of every bit of land in the city. That's how we trace the history of old homes."

Parcel maps? I'd seen a parcel map number and a diagram on the title to our bungalow, but it never occurred to me that magic elves spent their entire lives puzzling together every clod of dirt into Los Angeles maps. With earthquakes, fires, drought and rains, the land shifted constantly. I thought friendly fences defined homes and neighborhoods, not these thin lines of ink drawn around every inch of property or county land. Oh well, why not look at one and see what I could learn?

Los Angeles County Hall of Records, a sixties modern edifice full of mummies, houses dusty old papers bound into enormous books, faded ink drawn into stories of the land. I looked up the address in a book that spanned the early twentieth century. "Rancho San Rafael" whatever that was. San Rafael Avenue with its stately homes and shade trees ran across the top of our hill. That had absolutely nothing to do with the land I saw. The map showed hundreds of acres of blank space. No picture of a house on that map.

More books. Still no house, and I was now reading into the

war years. Just one more volume and I'd quit for the day. I flipped page after page when an image appeared. The map looked right, the shape of the house looked right, but how did a 1910 house land in the canyon in 1953? Thirty-five acres and an improvement, deeded to A. P. Coviello, an entertainment lawyer.

The address did not match. A faded lintel over the front door exposed the numerals 523, a number that did not exist in our neighborhood streets. Did addresses change with the growth of the city? The parcel map gave the address: 1550 Bridgeport.

My mind strayed to the rooms in the old house with those nasty wall-to-wall carpets, pink and black kitschy wallpaper, Formica counters, aluminum shower doors. I'd seen these colors in my friends' homes—1950s interior décor. Preservationists call this "remuddling." Fortunately, no one ever painted over the woodwork or the bricks. Buckets of mint green paint once set off the warm tones of the teak. Rooms now stood dark and faded, ashes swept from the bricks and dirty copper chandeliers stowed away in our garage.

December days grew short. I had to pick up Eric from the sitter. Clearly I'd spend another day at County Hall of Records.

At the Hall of Records, notebooks in hand, I once again climbed the stairs into the great hall, got directions down toward the basement, then the subbasement. The windowless subbasement resembled a hospital morgue. Bare lights and concrete hallways, passages into rooms and rooms of more books recorded in impeccable penmanship.

I wonder if the Chinese man who greeted me down there had seen another human in weeks. He looked terribly shy, had a slightly bowed back, thick glasses and graying hair. Then he smiled.

"You want to find out about a house? I can help with that. What's the address?"

He began clearing the stack of books on his desk.

I didn't know the address. I only knew about the darkened numbers on the lintel, surrounded by faded wood.

"I think we can find an address from those numbers. The record says 1952-53, correct? Let's go to those record books and find out if someone had taken off a house from the tax rolls at that time, with that address."

I pored over the new books and found 523 South Kingsley, sold for taxes in 1952. How sad. Life in Los Angeles presents a quilt of fortunes, money made, money spent, families grown, families vanished. Someone had to vacate their beautiful home in 1952, and again in 1982, a family dream shattered. This house had sheltered at least two families and now she stood alone again, less than thirty years later.

So, who were these people?

"Oh, we don't keep records for people here. For that you will need to go to the public library." My guide to the underworld scuttled back into the catacomb of shelves with the big books. A magic dot drawing formed in my notebook.

"How do I find out who built a house before 1910?"

The library archivist took me up to a lovely private reading room, heavy oak tables, comfortable chairs. High windows, beamed ceilings, and all the gorgeous mission tilework that characterizes 1930s Los Angeles public buildings. The federal government employed hundreds of artisans to build a city that would nod to the future as well as pay homage to the Spanish past. Heavy wood, sunlight, books—may heaven be like this.

Two boxes of fragile paperbacks sat on the table in front of me. Absolute silence. I whispered *thank you*. My hands clean, I pulled the first volume of a magazine called *Southern California Builder and Contractor*. Found permits issued to build a home at 523 S. Kingsley Street in downtown Los Angeles, with construction commencing October 9, 1908, and approved for occupancy May 15, 1909, in a modern neighborhood bordered by Wilshire Boulevard, a new gathering place for the carriage trade.

City tax records indicated a cost of $6,500 when a nice home in the area ran about $4,000-5,000. The permits didn't list an architect's name alongside the contractor, Mr. Wiechman. Most Craftsman homeowners selected a pattern from a Sears Roebuck catalog and ordered plans or perhaps a kit to assemble the house. In this case, the custom details and specialized hardwoods of this house, indicated a custom home.

I phoned Dr. Winter again.

"Bob, I've spent three days digging through records, but I think we have a problem."

"What is your worry?" Bob knew we didn't have the money or expertise to save the house, but he supported our efforts to get the salvage operation under way.

"I couldn't turn up any records on Louis Easton. We don't know if he ever went near this property. Doesn't that gum up our protective status?"

"No, not really. Easton wasn't a registered architect and his name didn't appear on building permits. You've done the research that the commission needs, and the house has proved significant. Everyone wants to make sure you find a way to save this beauty."

"I learned a little about the people who had it built. I found a name: Herman Flatau, businessman."

Modern carriage trade homes lay closer to downtown, in the

area now called Westlake. In my mind's eye a bowler hatted man got on the streetcar each day, rode to his downtown office, greeted his workers. Except that Mr. Flatau had a business as a grocery whole-saler in a town where horses and carts brought in milk cans from the Gilmore dairy farms out by Third and Fairfax. On Saturdays they likely attended the Temple B'nai B'rith, now known as the Wilshire Temple, a ten-minute walk from the house. According to Los Angeles city records, Frances Bernstein Flatau was the first woman to graduate a Los Angeles high school and enroll in the University of California, attaining a Ph.Bachelor. Moneyed, educated and modern in their thinking, the Flateaus represented a force for the new city.

They raised a family of three boys and one girl, all resting in Forest Lawn.

Months later (4/29/86) the Los Angeles library fire destroyed the only copies of the building records.

The old house captured our neighborhood's interest. No mil-lionaires yet, but others began to help us figure out her secrets. An elderly fellow explained that people moved houses in the 1950s to accommodate the expanding city. Apartments and freeways replaced gracious houses of a past era.

We heard about school field trips to the old ranch, of animals and farmworkers, of sighting cowboy movie stars riding their horses. Now peach trees blossomed but green and brown nubs of fruits fell to the ground. Thousands of wildflowers grew in the stable yard, a thirty-year collection of recycled straw and manure.

I held Eric's hand as Don led us through a collection of old plows and harrows, sharp rusted points and edges half buried in the dirt, a bottomless black incinerator. Memo to self: Supervise the child with great care out here. Maybe we'd get Eric a hard hat and work boots, how cute would that be?

I bought two hard hats. The boy and I looked great in yellow, suited us well.

# CHAPTER SEVEN

# REAL LIFE
## JANUARY 1986

Cereal bits scattered on the laminate table, a few drops of spilled milk and a chortling little boy. Except for the money, not a bad way to start the day. Grabbed the phone off the kitchen wall when it began to ring.

"Connie, Patti B. I know it's pretty early your time."

Patti B., VP National Sales of the company that absorbed my former employer. I'd interviewed with her months ago, she more straightforward than I expected. Nothing came of that.

"I'm in Chicago. I've got a mess on my desk, client bids coming due and no time to get these proposals out. Can you do it?"

Me? Interested in a dream job?

"So, what do you want me to do?"

"If you can help us, I'll call our office manager and tell her you're coming in. Unlock my office, sort out the packets of proposals and figure out timelines and resources. I'll call again later. All confidential information and, by the way, I'm not authorized to hire anyone. They make all those decisions in Houston."

A great job with a promotion. Holy cow! Babysitter, check. Shoulder pad suits in dry cleaning bags, check. Silks of all colors to tie around my neck, check. Tame my mop to fit into an Aqua Net helmet. No car. Have to rent a horse until I'm back in the race. The eighties race, still a man's game, and women needed to look *all business*.

"One more thing, when you have the plans in order for clients, you have to talk to our Chief Financial Officer in Houston, a guy named John. Everything we do with money has to be approved by him. He'll probably ask for a non-disclosure. We'll figure out the rest in two weeks when I'm back in California."

In a flash, life looked good again. Geoff moved ahead with foundation plans and inquiries into permits, so the big house would prove either a folly or a dream that might come true. The fate of the old house lay in Geoff's hands for now.

After two pay stubs I could go buy a car. Knew exactly what I wanted. Sailed into the dealership and picked it out, negotiated a price.

The salesman looked at my paperwork, then the two stubs.

"That's pretty heavy bread for a chick."

Good Lord, I'd been warned that banks, men in charge, considered women suspect when it comes to credit. Guys didn't know that I, a female, shouldn't be paid a man's salary. For the past seven years I'd existed as a set of initials to disguise my gender. Didn't give a damn about the car salesman. Glendale's got about a hundred car dealers, but the little blue Sentra stared at me. Ignored the guy.

Don and I would need lots of money, and soon. The fantasy house non-compliant, not acceptable for any type of occupancy. Geoff worked on the blueprints. Without the engineering plan, Geoff's drawings counted only as pictures. We needed an engineer to determine loads and capacities in the structure, whether the old house could even be moved. Moved where? The engineer needed geological reports. Why a geologist? A geological conditions study would determine the route up the hill and the new placement of the house. Ka-ching! Four thousand dollars for core samples of earth, seismic reports and all sorts of notes on things like "expandable soil" whatever that means.

Geology to me meant cutting a few cool fossils out of a hillside, maybe exploring gems and minerals. Residential geology? All about dirt. Forty years ago Angelenos could build a house anywhere they wanted. Eric loved watching giant Tonka trucks come into our yard, drill, scream, and extrude the core samples. Geologists ruled.

Of course each of these three plans needed to be approved by a different cubicle of city hall, signed and stamped, before Geoff's plan could be finalized. Los Angeles Building and Safety opened at 7:00, so I could come in with my bundles of blueprints and spiral bound reports, jostle in line with work booted contractors and beg for stamps. Run for the elevators and then rush though bumper to bumper traffic to the office.

Might have been better if I'd just gotten pregnant again. The approval cycle took nine months and thousands of dollars in reports. Not one contractor bid in the files yet. Everything contingent on where we'd move, how we'd move, and what would be needed to reset the house. Forget permits. Permission to do what?

For a mother/builder, the strangest things become routine. Up in the dark, suit, pantyhose and slippers, apron. Set up breakfast. Then, lipstick, earrings and heels. Check briefcase before heading at a dead run for Building and Safety.

Outside pocket—three bound copies of Geo reports, ready to approve at Grading Division. A roll of blueprints. Inside pockets, a hundred-page government contract Request for Proposal, read and annotated at night, a daily planner, appointment calendar, and two to three yellow legal pads. Center pocket, the one for personal items? Wadded tissues, mints, receipts, a couple of Happy Meals action figures. Oh, I found the grocery list. A few hairpins. Locked into place where a normal person would have their keychain? My Swiss Army knife. Never ever without it. It can fix computers, cut nails, pick teeth. On a blistering hot August afternoon, I went into a gas station bathroom and cut my sweaty bangs with the miniature scissors, tired of drips in my eyes.

Our sales team landed the largest accounts in the history of the industry, corporations spending tens of millions with us. Stacks of client requests gathered in my office, with due dates at the beginning of November. On October 31, buzzing phone and red lights created distraction. I hadn't been to the coffee room for Halloween cupcakes, and I didn't want to speak with anyone, including our sales reps.

"Connie, it's Pat." My neighbor on the line.

"There's a bunch of kids in your house. At least thirty. Maybe more." She'd called police more than an hour ago, no response. I phoned Don. We both took early lunch, raced home. Changed shoes and picked up the radios and two mechanical screwdrivers.

Noise from our house, a couple cars parked below. Kids on the patio. Because of the weekly spray jobs, we knew the gang members by name, as well as the names of the more innocent "party" gangs. Dammit, we'd boarded up the house. How the hell did they get in?

Don moved downhill toward our plywood boards. The nails were ripped out. Some little bastards were able to lift them off. We had screws in our pockets, and within minutes we'd bolted the perpetrators inside the house. We waited for the police.

A bunch of boys fled by jumping off the second story balcony, but they didn't run into the path of arriving squad cars. The officers looked around, admired Don's presence of mind with the screwdrivers, commented.

"Sorry, we can't do anything. You aren't posted for 'No Trespassing.'"

Don and I looked at each other. We'd bought a good dozen signs. Showed the police our "NO TRESPASSING" signs tossed on the ground, replaced by PARTY signs on the posts.

The girls, and one boy in a cast stayed locked in. While two officers gathered names, Don, the Disciplinary Dean, conducted interviews.

"Ladies, do you really think you should go out with boys who will leave you stranded like this?"

When an officer came up my side of the hill, I suggested that the police keep an eye out for kids with sore feet who looked lost on the wrong side of the mountain. With that, I dashed back to the office.

That afternoon the house had to suffer an additional indignity, prosecution impossible because the property wasn't properly posted. The **No Trespassing** signs lay in the dirt, covered with tire tracks. Don spray painted two-foot high block letters that announced, "NO TRESPASSING" all over the exterior of the house, front, back, sides, upstairs and down.

# CHAPTER EIGHT

# BEGGED, BORROWED, STOLEN

Nobody funds mortgages for the high-risk process of moving and restoring a house. We had a mortgage on our existing home and made our expenses paycheck to paycheck. If we could get the house onto the new lot, we could then get financed as a "rehab" project at a very high interest rate. We needed cash and know-how.

Spreadsheets and flow charts filled the first binder. The cycle of preliminary reports became contractor bids—house mover, hillside excavation, foundation contractor. Major expenses to get a hundred tons of scrap lumber lifted, moved, and set down. The house mover proposed cutting the structure in in half, warned us that we would lose all the plaster and pipes. Mechanical systems for water, power, heating would need to be replaced. How much does that cost? Estimate, estimate, estimate.

Don and I could plaster and paint. Cover the graffiti. Rocks had gone through every last pane of glass. We'd learn how to replace glass in the windows. Beyond that, both of us clueless. Yes, I'd grown up working in old houses, but my skills set stopped after cosmetic.

Actually, I'd resisted learning mechanicals, my brother's territory. At sixteen I had to help Uncle Jack do an engine overhaul in exchange for driving lessons.

"Oh, I can't really do this. You know the women in this family aren't very mechanical."

Gentle Jack's eyes blazed behind the goggles. "Dammit Missy, there is no reason to believe that you are any less mechanical than any man in this family, and we are all engineers. Now hand me that wrench." Time to learn how to use that wrench, literally and figuratively. Know when to force things, when to ease up, and how to change directions.

The total estimate to achieve a Certificate of Occupancy would be, give or take, $200,000 with the stipulation that contractors had to have the work accomplished in one year, to meet finance company deadlines. Errors? Delays? Contingencies? Good luck with that. The absolute maximum mortgage that we could afford would be $200,000 a fair price for Los Angeles houses in 1986.

All this doable? Unlikely.

Don and Chuck liked the idea of the big house for all of us and so we spent several weekends together discussing the opportunity. Five bedrooms offered privacy for everybody. The nursery would make a great family room. We'd do the labor side by side. Chuck still had a full shop and Eric would grow up like my brother and me. When Chuck grew more senior, he'd have a secure home with his family. Chuck mortgaged his house.

We opened escrow. Downey Savings championed the idea of saving the big house and earning goodwill in the neighborhood. They drew up an offer for the land, a double lot for $60,000 and a house at no charge. The lot would be tied to our existing lot in something called a lot line adjustment. This idea used often when people want a bigger driveway or an appraisal. The movers would have to set the old house right on the new parcel before escrow closed. This timeline would keep the developers out of city hell. Sounded so crazy, maybe all that could work.

Bills and housework piled up. Both Don and I worked long hours. He took on extra duties at school from 6:00 a.m. donut runs to Friday night football games. With two big jobs we might be able to make this deal work.

The flu struck, not really a bad thing. After a couple days in bed wandered to the dining room table in the middle of the afternoon, set down my mug of tea. Opened up the first one of my personal bills, retail, a minimum payment, not too bad. Car payment, check. Utilities, then the phone bill. With more than fifty calls made to a number in Redondo Beach, thirty miles across town. Must be an error—2:30 a.m., 3:45 a.m. What the hell?

I called Don at school. "Hi babe, what's up?"

"Don, I found a whole bunch of toll calls to Redondo Beach, in the middle of the night."

"I'll be right home."

So began his long excuse about a "friend" at work–seeing some "Christian" lady who didn't think he should leave his family over her.

"It's kind of like your friendship with John." I thought about that for a moment. John lived in Texas, had a long-term marriage. We did travel together to meet major clients, and we had become close friends. Work friendships have barriers you don't cross because others will be hurt.

"So, have you been fucking her?"

"A few times."

I grabbed a tissue. Not sure if I wanted to deal with the stomach cramps or the tears first.

"How long has this been going on?"

"Maybe nine months."

*Damn him.* In other words, it began when I collapsed in grief over losing my uncle, overwhelmed with work and company travel, and complained about flying in on Thursday nights to pizza boxes and beer bottles.

I worked on a team of men who cared about me and my son. They understood the rules. Lionesses were allowed in the executive ranks and we knew how to hunt. Disruption of the home front? A tribal taboo.

Don crossed those lines. He drank after school, passed out by 7:00, then got up and drank more, vodka this time, and called his "friend" in the middle of the night after we were asleep, claiming that she rose at 3:00 every morning.

Don borrowed his dad's total equity after he got involved with this woman. We had a very expensive hole in the ground containing Chuck's life savings and not much else. No idea what to do now.

Clearly, we were going to need some serious marriage counseling. Don claimed he wanted to stay married, but he wanted *friends*. He had always mocked his parents' devotion to each other. Chuck embodied fierce love. He and Don's mom had been together since age twelve, a couple of cousins from Crab Orchard, Kentucky, until cancer parted them.

Don understood nothing about family love. How could this even be possible? His idea of the perfect woman, a sister-friend-lover. He never had a sister. We got to the first session with Victor who asked Don, "What can you tell me about your mother?"

"I don't know. How's yours?"

Shit. My dime, and he wouldn't talk or listen.

My models were mixed as well. I'd seen the brilliance of new expectations, the difficulties of daily work, and the dark betrayals and disappointments. Both my mother and grandmother had known love, and neither recommended it. My uncles were wonderful to me, but they were gay.

So here we were, in this strange wandering relationship. I trusted the men I worked with. Don? What's love without trust?

We stayed polite to each other, considerate even. Don brought home a vegetarian pizza. Later in the evening a bottle of Chianti stood open on the large stereo speakers that we used for end tables. Eric snuggled all safe in bed with a full tummy and his pile of stuffed animals, down quilt rumpled into a blue cloud. Plenty of love, all about the boy. We would make sure he could depend on the two of us, no matter what.

Ugh.

Chuck stepped back from our problems. He began to struggle with illness, eventual colon cancer, but not enough to send him to his departed wife. Somewhere in this, he'd decided to give up his constant companion, an African Grey parrot named Jack.

The bird had some 200 phrases, and he knew how to speak in context. If someone went into the bathroom, the parrot would gurgle toilet-flushing sounds.

Jack picked up all conversations—nice and not so nice. The strain sat there, grew. No fighting in front of the boy.

Me? Nauseous all the time, and no, not with a little brother or sister. Our vegetarian diet consisted of a lot of pasta with vegetables. Turns out that I had an undiagnosed allergy to tomatoes, sensitive to wheat as well. Double ugh. The bottom line to all this we began our mornings with Don hung over, me queasy.

Don snarled and yelled at everything, I muttered. The damned bird heard me once too often. One morning Don stormed out the door, coffee thermos in hand. The parrot responded, "Get out, just get out!"

Don came running back to the door, said, "Parrot found strangled—film at 11!"

We both collapsed, laughed, hugged.

## APRIL 1987

"Hon, I know you're at Victors. Did you do something with your jewelry?" By now Don decided he didn't need counseling. I could go, and if I really hated the drinking, I could go to Al-Anon meetings.

"No." My therapist picked up his phone and handed it to me.

"I think you better come home."

My jewelry box lay open, on my bed, stripped of my rings—grandmother's wedding ruby, a filigreed garnet that celebrated my college graduation. Every day for the past eight years I wore my twelve-carat cabochon sapphire—a gorgeous, brilliant blue. My mother bought that ring for me when we visited China, a gift to let me know everything would be okay between us, forever. That morning I left the house at 3:00 a.m. in pursuit of a massive defense account. Draft materials needed to arrive in time for a morning meeting, Houston time. Even though a scarf and earrings were de rigueur for casual wear, I crept away in a velour jumpsuit, bare of jewelry.

The sapphire, gone. Our wedding rings, gone—we'd put them aside for a few weeks while we investigated the contents of our hearts and had our heads examined by a professional. Gone also, a hundred-ducat double eagle coin that I wore most days, the flash of gold somehow an icon for winning big games.

The robbery left us shaken. Even though my treasures didn't count as cash in the bank, many pieces of the gold jewelry marked sentiments or achievements, the way I presented myself to a world that often felt beyond my reach.

Don called the police and showed a pair of sunglasses that somebody dropped beside the dog door. City tree contractors had been by that day. The phone rang. Our storage unit. "Someone broke the locks on your unit." Of course. The damn card sat in my jewelry box.

Stolen property, actually everything I owned of value except our house. A marriage and family threatened by predatory women and a clueless husband. Oh, and we had a massive house down in the canyon, uninsured and open to vandals and arsonists. It represented a $60,000 debt to my father-in-law.

A couple days later I broke down, sobbed until I choked. Don, gone again. Got into the bathtub, try to soften anxiety with bubbles. Little Eric opened the door, picked up the big sponge, started washing my back.

"Don't cry, Mommy."

Soaked the sponge again. Smoothed it down my shaking back.

"Calm down, Mommy."

Got out of the tub, grabbed Eric and fled to my mother in San Diego, no note.

When I got back to LA, a huge arrangement of wilted flowers sat on the dining room table. My stomach heaved, followed by the lungs—no air–everything inside me filled with liquid—couldn't breathe.

Days later Don and I met at Victor's. Don fancied himself as a clever and witty foil to this intrusive counseling nonsense. He preferred endless rounds of emotional judo. I came out of them the worse for wear, bruised, scraped, teeth grinding. Victor asked him about the court order to attend AA.

"I hate it. The people are weird. The place stinks, and it's the same fundamentalist bullshit I grew up on."

Work fatigue set up a critical juncture on this April evening.

Victor may have been tired of Don's joking and hedging. "What do you think? Do you want to stay married, or do you want to go?"

I held my breath. Do men marry us out of lust, and then stay around out of pity? For weeks I'd wondered, "What is happily married for a man?" Don shrugged his shoulders.

"I don't care—either way is fine. There's the boy, Chuck's money in the big house..."

My head snapped around. "I'll give you a forty-five-minute head start."

"What?"

"We're fifteen minutes into this session. When I get home, I want you gone."

*Two hearts in fragile outline shapes*
*Twisted beyond recognition*
*Tossed into the crucible.*
*Waiting for the torch.*

# CHAPTER NINE

# LOOSE FOOTING

"Connie, if I were younger or stronger, I'd horsewhip him."
My father-in-law on the phone with me.

"I never spanked him. He always did as he pleased." Chuck's generosity and heart, his adoration of Don and Eric, unquestioned. For the first time he reached out to me, Eric's mother. I sat in my pajamas and listened.

The unexpected call, his confidence saddened me. Chuck at least as upset about Don's affairs as I, maybe even more so.

"I don't know what to say. My mother had ten children. When we buried Pappy, she didn't cry. She looked down at the grave and said, 'At least now I know where he is.'" Comforting to share the hurt and anger? Definitely enlightening.

Over the years I'd heard a litany, Chuck constantly worrying about his health, and the inevitability that one day he'd join Don's mother in heaven, his push-me/pull-you relationship with death. This gentle man wanted us to somehow reconcile, but at the same time, he made it clear that he understood the betrayal of a family.

That call meant a lot to me. I could have walked away from Don and from our hole in the ground.

The dream continued. Fantasy has a way of overriding reality.

Geoff and I conceived our idea for the home as a long elegant front yard, somewhat secluded, with a path of California live oaks or cypress trees leading to the front door. Wrong. Turned out that the location I'd chosen consisted of expandable soil, and I soon learned what that meant. Dry adobe fills with water and becomes sludge. During winter storms the slippery clay destabilizes, slides downhill. The farther down the hillside you go, the more expandable soil, a years' long collection of mud.

At the top of the hill, near the street we had only a foot to bedrock. This structure of California hills explains the expense of homes in hilltop neighborhoods. Houses must be set into rock instead of loose soil that shifts with rains or any seismic action.

Now we needed to hire a surveyor. What next? That morning Geoff and the surveyor measured out a lot that could be drilled right into the rock. Now for a grading contractor. Not sure how we found Joe, but what a godsend.

Joe looked at the elevation studies on the blueprints.

"Did they tell you, you need a keyway?"

The grading estimate? $40,000, plus another $40,000 to move the house. Escrow wouldn't close on the $60,000 lot until we moved the house in place.

The Caterpillars arrived, a large tractor bulldozer, and a big wheeled one with a tamping plate.

I'd never heard of a keyway. The soils report showed loose soil at the bottom of our lot. When it rains, gravel and decomposed granite run downhill, right over the slipcoat of mud. If you walk down loose soil in your hiking boots, the grit and pebbles slide underneath your feet. That's where the wildflowers grow but you don't want to drive your car on it.

The solution? Stabilize the bottom of the new lot. A trench fifteen feet wide and eight feet deep had to be excavated across the entire hundred-foot base. Then we'd need to build the world's largest adobe block. For two weeks, the bulldozers roared in the canyon. They scooped up all the adobe they could find. Each couple of days two feet of adobe went in. Kids borrowed neighbors' garden hoses and stood in the sun wetting the soil until they had clay that could be formed and compacted with heavy equipment. The dozer rolled back and forth over the clay, then the 2x15x100-foot block baked in the sun. A soils inspector would visit, take a sample, and okay us for the next layer.

We had to build a road, one with the soil and rock dense enough to take a hundred-ton house. For weeks Caterpillar tractors scraped, rammed, and rolled the canyon into a suitable surface to transport a hundred-ton house. The earth vibrated until people's teeth fell out. Instead of complaining, the neighbors lent garden hoses and kids to moisten the soil, water the transplanted trees. In order to drag a hundred-ton house up the hillside, the road would have to take the weight. The hilltop consisted of solid bedrock, about eighteen inches from the surface.

Everybody got a turn to ride on the bulldozer. On the sides of the trench lay all the uprooted trees and vegetation as well as two stray dogs and five bathtubs.

The house would have to be much closer to the street than planned, and we dug the new pad as well as jackhammered a narrow trench about four feet deep to hold the deadman posts. Deadman posts are used as braces for the pulley system. The twelve by twelve hardwood timbers are thicker than a phone pole. After five thousand years of lifting heavy things, man has not come up with a stronger substance than a tree. Pulley wheels and winch cables are slung around the posts to secure the load.

For eight years, Don had called me a "wench" a simple sobriquet for a Renaissance Faire performer. I now wore a new T-shirt with "WINCH" printed across my chest.

The bank sent out press releases and NBC came out to film the gifting of the house. Downey Savings wanted to see a happy ending to the story. The newscaster explained how that bank had a chance to help save a piece of classic architecture for the community. The gang activity on site threatened the entire neighborhood. Solution? Donate the home for restoration.

Don showed up for the press event, nattered on how the move would happen. For the camera, he played the star, climbed all over the place, spouted an imaginary encyclopedia of house preservation. Don lived in a 1950s apartment. Somehow the dream survived.

# CHAPTER TEN

# MOVIN' ON
## JULY 1987

I'd staked every borrowed cent on the actions of these next few days. Escrow was about to close on a $60,000 parcel of land. Don ready to sign paperwork, but not willing to invest another moment or cent in the project.

Sleepless nights dissolved into dreams of work, numbers on client projects whirling through my head, as well as the numbers on my mounting debt. A little child snoring beside me as I worried. Nervous exhaustion and endless pots of coffee kept things going from daybreak until past midnight, week after week. I had no idea what to do, too driven by the tasks to take time for anxiety attacks. Too anxious to be afraid of what comes next.

Exactly how did I get to that point? Good question. It seemed as if the house were dragging me and all these workers up the hill instead of vice versa. She spoke to me, day after day—pleading, cajoling, instructing. I needed a house whisperer, someone who could understand a building's soul, and I knew who to call.

My childhood best friend, Andee, a curly haired sprite with unlimited stamina. As little girls on bicycles riding around our home town, we drew Victorian houses, barns and churches for days at a time. Carried lunches and sketchbooks, sometimes oil paints, in our bike baskets.

The only bicycle here whirled around in my mind, flipped

upside down, wheels spinning in the dirt and torn up roots. Grown up planners replaced sketchbooks with blocks for each part of the day, or a life. Just not this life.

Now a preservation architect, Andee had her own business. "Andee, if you can get a week off, I'll buy your plane ticket."

"When are you moving it?"

"Next week, on my birthday." The strangeness of this birthday gift, none of it planned.

"Gee, I'd love to film that."

We were on! Days later I slogged through LAX baggage claim to pick up a pert traveler with a backpack of jeans, T-shirts, and boots. One additional bag of professional camera equipment.

These days the neighbors and I became accustomed to the early morning sounds, grinding and roaring of the mover's trucks. A neighbor permitted us to tear down her fence and driveway to accommodate the vehicles, in exchange for a new driveway later in the summer. Two old men stood by the fence today, out for a crack of dawn walk with their dogs. One, a retired architect, the other a retired landscaper. Thankfully, both wanted to see the neighborhood landmark enter a new life. They often shared stories of people who came and went over the years, of wild parties that resonated through the canyon. One of the men commented, "House movers, boy, that's one rough crowd."

Heavy trucks roared up the canyon from below. Five muscle-bound workers jumped out to follow Mac, the team leader. They piled huge timbers into the hallway and living room. Chainsaws roared, cutting through the upstairs. Plaster cracked apart, tumbled through the oaken floors. As soon as one worker cut, two others grabbed a board and braced it against the arch. Sledgehammers pounded boards into X shapes, jammed everything into place until it couldn't budge. No nails. The forces of the building would hold all the parts together, unless something slipped.

Satisfied with that, a team of workers climbed under the house. They checked the knob and tube wiring for power, snipped every string. Huge wrenches bent plumbing pipes into strange alphabets, twisting until every piece of lead broke.

Saws cut through asbestos pipes. The men tore out all the ductwork until they could shove the old furnace out the back. "Lady, it probably still works. You'll be able to reinstall it later, so save it." My rubble mountain grew. Mechanical parts piled here, broken plaster there, and used bricks stacked up on the side.

Mac's whistle pierced the air.

"Need cribbing over here!"

"Cribbing?"

Big sticks, the size of railroad ties, six by six inches. A giant with brilliant blond hair and a red beard down to his chest unloaded timbers from a truck, each about five feet long. His massive arms whirled through the air tossing lumber at a smaller man. The wiry little guy dove under the foundation sills again and again, setting the lumber into crisscrossed stacks, like a child's toy. No nails, no mortar. Memo to self—get Eric a set of Lincoln Logs.

The feral cat and two dogs ran away from this cacophony of sledgehammers and chainsaws. No doubt even the rattlesnakes fled. The only question then, why didn't I run away?

Sparks and yelling. The house-mover's saws stopped at old steel straps and plates.

We all understood that the home had been moved in 1952, and that it had been cut then. Mac's decision, "Let's cut her in the same place." It turned out that cutting over an old seam is not a good idea. Instead of redwood, the old cut had been completely sealed and reinforced with heavy steel. They jigged around the plate.

The mind's eye doesn't really offer clear vision. There were no secrets in this process. No omissions. Somehow, I'd envisioned a house moving up the hill. Day after day contractors told me what they would need to do. I was there when the mason brought out a professional photographer before the move, counted up the courses of inlaid tapestry bricks. They drew plans, sourced bricks made of the same local clay. Demolition hadn't been in the picture.

The masonry was too heavy to move. The gorgeous teak living room? Dreams of a book in front of the fireplace? More sledgehammers. Masons banged on the bricks and knocked a huge hole in one side of the house. They claimed, "Ma'am, we can't move it with the fireplaces. This brick's gotta come down. Otherwise, when we tilt her to take her up the hill, that two-story chimney will rip her into scrap." Demolition for the house move topped anything any gang had ever attempted.

Today the workers were busting up her hearth, banging the existing fireplace to shards. I looked around at the flying dust and sharp debris.

"Please don't damage the woodwork!" They dropped their sledgehammers.

Andee and I quickly located canvas and plastic to cover the wood. Then we walked along the new split.

Andee exclaims, "Oooooh look! You can really see it, how it's made when a house pulls apart." She lifted her camera. "The views, breathtaking, the way you can see the canyon right through the house!" I'd never thought of this—the rend down the middle of the home made me cringe.

She refocused her camera. "Wow, look at this woodwork, these elaborate joints, the massive doors... How on earth did they find this lumber?"

For a few moments we didn't hear the din of workers, hammers, or saws.

Her voice again. "This house, so special, the thought and care... I can't imagine."

Andee heard the same voice I did. A need to save thousands

of hours of planning and designing something lovely, the care that went into making this beautiful home. To us, it was a living thing.

"Neither can I." We stood in the downstairs hallway, at the foot of an intricately joined banister.

Andee pulled out her flashlight and shined it on a clean stair banister. I'd washed and oiled it but never looked at it with the joiner's eye. She noted a carpenter's innovation. We started up the stairs to the mezzanine, a pleasant seating location with wide benches.

At the top stood a full nine by twelve-foot bank of leaded glass windows, bent apart by vandals. Shaped pieces of purple and green pulled away from clear plate with its slightly undulating surface, tiny bubbles in the panes. Those windows had been a work of art. Fortunately, I'd photographed them before vandals shattered the glass and bent the frames, hoped to restore them one day. This afternoon the smashed leaded glass tilted into the upstairs hallway. I picked up pieces of broken glass.

Andee and I gathered up ladders and tools, removed the remaining panes, numbered them and packed them between sheets of plywood. The big tin-lined bench offered safe storage for our stack of broken lead and colored glass. What's trash, and what's treasure? This wasn't the day to decide. By now I'd swept up the shattered glass from 103 broken windows. No idea how to fix them.

Evening sun began to stream through the blank frames.

# CHAPTER ELEVEN

# WHAT COULD POSSIBLY GO WRONG?

## JULY 1987

The fast pace, the dirt and the sense of anticipation raised our spirits. Many days I sensed my grandfather watching over us, heard his laughter. His words about challenge? "Dive in over your head, then work your way out of it." The months spent planning the flow of time and money all amounted to this, a huge, high risk move of an old building. Eric thrived in the chaos, watching a lot of "guys" roaring around on the world's biggest Tonka trucks.

After two weeks of sawing, movers got the pieces loaded onto dollies and turned the dollies toward the freshly compacted dirt road. The old patios were gone, shoved into a gaping hole in the ground. A dried-out peach orchard, its leaves and trunks far beyond the lifespan of blooming, hadn't fruited in years. The dozers snapped through it, then roared uphill, scooped up a pair of young black walnuts and set them into holes at the side, transplants.

This morning, four reconfigured semi-trailer trucks, each extending nearly forty feet long, parked across a twenty-two-foot wide street. Cement filled each trailer to a weight of twenty-six tons. That's what's needed to counterweight a hundred ton building on a hillside. The day would be a tug o' war between men and gravity.

I bet on the men. It was my birthday and a good day for a

win. Neighbors wandered onto my lot, adding to the coffeepot, the keg of beer and picnic supplies. Together we learned how they built Stonehenge—straining muscles, ropes and whistles. Simple physics at work, with all equipment made of sticks, lines and pulleys.

These men used the same forces, with the addition of big iron —tractors, bulldozers, compactors. Winch lines unwound from their pulleys. My new lot was a level pad, surrounded by eight-foot deep ditches, each only about eighteen inches wide. A series of twelve by twelve timbers set eight feet into the bedrock trench. Cables wrapped around a series of these "deadman" posts set to brace and hold the weight of the house.

Heavy equipment can't do it all. Men ran up and down the hill tugging the heavy cables and ropes, locked massive hooks into place on the trailers. Ingenuity and raw muscle.

Magic fairies completed the picture. A van from Eric's preschool pulled up, unloaded a dozen little kids from Eric's class, four-year-olds with two adults. We gave them juice and cookies, perched them in the limbs of a sturdy walnut tree.

The four trucks were ready to wind and haul. Engines growled, and winch lines whirred. A child exclaims, "Danger coming!" Right. A snapped cable could swipe us all out. The trucks at the top of the street screamed as winch lines strained against the weight of the structure. The throttles of the trucks keep lines taut and even. Whistles pierced the air as Mac watched and signaled the operators.

After months of preparation, the move up our 30 degree slope took less than two hours. The shorter half of the house was in place, an eerie sight with its half-bath, split bedrooms and the once gorgeous living room now boarded up.

*We celebrated into the night. I was now the proud owner of 100 tons of scrap lumber.*

Two weeks later half the house rested next to my bungalow, alone in the dirt, open and exposed. A bathroom mirror glared out at us, flocked wallpaper hanging off the broken plaster. The pink alcove bedroom, my imaginary place to read and sew, sawn through. The main hall stood cross braced with timbers. Doorways hovered some 12 feet in the air, stacked on loose lumber.

Morning sun and a clear sky, a hot day ahead. No breeze. Mac, the foreman, arrived at seven a.m. ready to do battle with heat and gravity.

The second part of the house lay down the hill, a long section, nearly twice the size of the piece we moved last week. The long half of the house wouldn't fit onto a single dolly. Five-ton I-beams now stretched across two dollies, supporting the structure. More big iron came rumbling down Avenue 37, ready to hoist.

Two neighbors sacrificed their driveways, contingent on my promises to replace their driveways and gates. Other residents, some on their way to work, drove down the little street, stopped at the road barrier. They could turn around and get off the other side of the hill, or park, stand at the fence and gape. Also at the fence, an intern Los Angeles Times reporter with his camera and notepad as well as a couple other newspeople. The coffeepot was on.

Winch lines let out all the way down to the dollies, more than 300 feet downhill. By mid-morning the sun was August hot, too hot to even perspire. Dusty workers checked the lines and locks, whistled commands. Engines groaned, wheels spinning up dirt. House movers don't talk much. Their eyes moved constantly, up and down the canyon, side to side as they watched each other, the vehicles, and the structure. We heard a crunch, then whistles from all the men. I gasped, and Mac glared at me.

Yes, my entire investment hung in jeopardy, and no, there was nothing I could do right then. An I-beam hit straight into the hill and jammed into the dirt. The off-balance truck skidded down and stalled near the keyway, on top of fine adobe dust. Tires whirred, ground deeper into their tracks. Only so much can be done with machinery, even heavy equipment. Clearly momentum was not our friend.

Solutions lie in simple physics. Mac points to the large walnut tree where Eric's pre-K class sat a week earlier to watch the first half of the house move. Now neighbors are ordered to stay fifty feet away from that tree. We crowd into the bungalow backyard, protected by a chain-link fence. How in the world will they pull that truck out with cables and a walnut tree?

Shouts and whistles. Sunburned backs and muscles straining, several men drag the cable uphill toward the tree, wrap it around the trunk, then guide it back downhill onto a second truck, hook it up to the pulley. A winch begins to wind, then scream, metal on metal. Will the weighted larger truck be enough to pull the dolly out of the silt? What if the tree snaps in two with the force? I actually didn't want to look. There's no insurance for an undertaking like this.

The gears crunched on. The slip—can they straighten out the visible leaning?

I turned to a friend. "It's still leaning! Will it go straight again when we set it down?"

He responded, "Oh man, if it doesn't you'll have to remove every single nail and rehang every door and window." The flapping windows and doors did not look promising.

The two dollies turned in sync with their load, inched it up the hill. Exhausted after nearly nine hours in progress, the house movers stacked up the cribbing, and set down the long side of the building, dining room, pantry, kitchen and the massive stairwell.

Those windows would never be exactly right. I walked around my prize.

Her two sides did not match. The long side sat six inches higher than the shorter side. She wasn't level, not even close.

# CHAPTER TWELVE

# CITY HELL

## AUGUST 1987

The old house sat on her new lot. Six months earlier, Don and I had opened escrow with a lot line adjustment, tied the new land to our bungalow. We bought the land, and the bank deeded us the house. The bank's advice on this had saved us the cost of permits and saved them the cost of refiling their parcel maps. The neighborhood zoned for "single family residence" was in full agreement with the strategy for saving the old house.

I marched into City Hall in my high heels and suit, ready to process my lot split. Once they untied the lots, we could sell the bungalow.

The same maze of cubicles and counters, gray blue carpeting, gray walls, people lined up with rolls of blueprints. Men in painters' whites arguing steps in the process, homeowners with hand drawn sketches for additions being sent away and told to come in with proper plans. Disappointments and grim faces leave the counters.

Our house sat in place, escrow closed. We'd have a foundation in a couple months and then I could start work on the interior. At the counter I asked for the papers to apply for a lot split, took them to a table, filled everything out and attached all my documents before blasting out HWY 101 to be in my office by 8:30. This would be a necessary step to selling the bungalow, and to getting even a temporary Certificate of Occupancy. Both issues pressed. The bungalow had a mortgage and the big house must become habitable in three short months.

Two weeks later a four-page letter arrived by mail, single spaced technical comments. I called Geoff and Otto for a meeting.

"What are 'Conditions'?" I asked. The architect and engineer frowned as they looked at the letter:

- Remove overhanging eaves from house
- Cut off all extended beams
- Remove wooden windows and replace with aluminum or plastic
- Stucco over cedar shingles
- Install sprinkler systems inside and out

Nothing supported the restoration work. The fire department wanted us to destroy the Craftsman features of the home. Whatever happened to the input from the Cultural Heritage Commission, the august body who had encouraged me to go ahead with saving the house?

There was more—in fact a total of twenty-one items that had nothing to do with saving the house. This next group from Public works was a total puzzlement.

- Widen the street to regulation
- Excavate and fill the edge of the street on both sides
- Pour concrete sidewalks and curbs
- Install 2 streetlights

Each department of the city had added three to four standard developer's conditions to their wish lists. Street planning wanted a new road instead of our existing streets.

There was no way to separate the title on my little bungalow until the items in this letter cleared, but each item cost more than I'd already spent. The city wanted public works improvements to the tune of some $300,000. What happened? I went down to Building and Safety, City Planning office.

Here's what I understood. Everyone in City Hell had a private fiefdom with a moat, and a portcullis concealing the lions, tigers and bears. Some counters appeared benevolent, some offered to help and then gave every reason why they could do nothing. Others covered errors and created excuses.

The meanest and toughest of all the pocket protector men exited his lair. He'd obstructed Downey Savings for years, denied one parcel map after another, originally in response to the complaints of neighbors who did not want to see excessive development near their high end homes. He didn't look up from the counter at me. He didn't look at the letter, or at the existing maps for the area.

"No."

"I don't understand. No, what?"

"We're not waiving any of these restrictions."

My new lot sat at the edge of an old parcel map, filed by Downey Savings, along with their plans for a development of 80 homes. Their renderings illustrated a planned community of streets and cul de sacs, stucco houses, several small streets and all the modern amenities. It didn't matter to him that I was a private resident. It mattered a lot to me that I could not put my bungalow up for sale.

"But we're not adding anything new to the neighborhood. We just want to restore the old farmhouse." I looked across at the planned neighborhood. "That's not even my street."

"Lady, as far as I'm concerned, Killarney Avenue's just a high-class alley, and yes, it's up to residents to improve the street."

I pleaded with him to have someone, anyone come out and walk the neighborhood with me. Kids could play outside until dark or walk to friend's houses on Mt. Washington. Families had block parties, no driving. Someone made an awful mistake. I called on my

City Council member. The aide took a look at the document, then left the room. Not a good sign, no words of reassurance.

Tears flowed by the time I reached the parking lot, pulled out tissues and my parking stub. The attendant claimed overtime on my parking permit by six minutes. "Pay $15.00." I didn't have it. He reached into my car window to grab my keys. My nails went into the back of his hand, he yelped, and I tore out of the lot.

# CHAPTER THIRTEEN

# FOUNDATION
## FALL, 1987

That fall I wondered if we bring disasters on ourselves, or if they just find us? For some reason I rolled into calamities like a puppy on a chew toy. Building and Safety challenges ended our little ritual of breakfasts. Thankfully, the babysitter fed Eric on City Hell mornings.

Went to work, put my head under a tsunami of contract bids and returned calls to our national sales force of some twenty-one account executives. Appearance: try and look normal; this is nobody's business. Kicked off the high heels under my desk, and stretched toes against taut pantyhose, suit jacket and scarf over the back of a chair in case I needed to present myself on quick notice.

At midday I popped open the Tupperware of tuna salad, or "Mommy's Kitty Queen" as Don called my lunches. Time for the daily update, an adult conversation with Faye, lifetime best friend.

We'd come a long way together, both owned landmark houses on Mt. Washington, a bohemian area of northeast LA. I had my little boy, and she'd moved her mother into the back house on her lot. While sane adults broke for a quick soap opera in the lunch room, Faye and I narrated our own. Faye went first.

"I had to take mother's leg into the orthopedist today."

"Say what?" At eighty Marjorie, still a pretty lady, her wigs on straight and her makeup set, but wheelchair bound. In 1987 reliable knee replacements weren't available and the option was to replace an arthritic leg with a prosthetic limb.

"One of her lovers broke it when he tried to take it off."

I dropped my fork, splashing salad dressing on a silk blouse. It took a couple minutes to clear up the coughing.

"Jesus, she has to take her leg off too? She still seeing all three of those guys?"

Faye started laughing. "Everybody needs a hobby."

Both Faye and I had tired of men, admired Marjorie for her persistence, an object lesson for us all.

"Sounds better than my morning. I'm gonna kill Mudd. He's got cement for brains."

On to the trials of the old house. Faye and I shared dreams of possibilities for our Mt. Washington treasure.

My first vision of it—a comfortable hearth, a family home. Hers, an elegant party venue, a place for everyone on the mountain to enjoy if we would only put it back together. Why not both? The optimist in Faye saw polished hardwood underneath shattered and dry rotted bits. My reality? Deadlines loomed, or there'd be overcharges for delays and the mover's equipment. Impossible to begin work on the house until the movers set it into a foundation. It needed to be rehabbed and legal for occupancy before the balloon payment due date.

We griped, both upset with Mudd, the foundation contractor from hell. He'd done decent work on her home. Mudd's bid came in at $40,000 and we sealed it over a beer and a check. He scheduled the work so that the foundation would be complete, house set down and roof closed by the time the winter rains came. "We'll be set down by October, maybe November at the latest."

Why did building the foundation come after relocating the house?

Turned out, Mudd had no idea what he was doing. He knew how to pour concrete and leave a few holes for pipes. Let a builder figure out how to put in the mechanical systems, going from the ground up. Mudd had never done a move-on; how hard could that be?

The process to build the foundation underneath the cribbed house is exactly reversed from a new house. Existing houses are working systems of pipes, large ducts for heating, plumbing systems that have to eventually hook up to the streets and sewers, electrical conduit, you name it. Power lines have to come down to junction boxes, tie into city power poles. Pipes have to run to the sewer system. The architect designs a foundation built so that all the pipes and tubes running under the house will match up to city utilities. Except the contractor has to actually look at the architect's drawings and follow the plans.

The sound of jackhammers in the morning reassured me. Mudd seemed to understand the job he'd bid on. Our new foundation would sit like a tooth, rooted into the deep trenches dug for the deadman posts. Footings jackhammered into bedrock tapered to match the hillside. Dirt heaped up beside the 18" footings at the back. Rebar and blocks arrived.

Everything under control, payments cleared. I had airline passes from work so Eric and I took a ten-day vacation to my Tante Sophia in Amsterdam. We climbed four story ladders up inside of windmills and visited miniature villages. Examined the pulley system in our 17th century family home—one designed to lift a grand piano off a barge. For some odd reason the kid obsessed with structures. His four-year-old mind queried constantly, "How does this work?" about everything from the gear systems in Dutch wall clocks to the dikes holding back the North Sea. If it had moving parts, he loved it.

We returned from Holland in mid-September, set down our bags, and ran across the yard, expecting to see our nearly complete foundation. No workmen had visited the site since the Friday before we left. Old lunch wrappers lay in place on the ground, soda cans tossed aside. Jet lagged and angry, I called Mudd.

Progress slowed to a crawl. Instead of beginning at 7:00, they showed up later in the mornings, long after Eric and I had taken off for day care and work. When we came home at night, a few blocks stacked on the rebar, and damp mortar let me know that something happened on that day.

Met them with a smile the day they showed up on time.

"Oh, I don't have the materials today. We can work if you can come with me to the brickyard." Mudd hadn't paid his suppliers. I'd paid for the next phase of work and he couldn't buy the concrete. A new 7:00 errand, visit the local lumberyards and use my Visa to order concrete.

The three little pigs had nothing on this mess of large-scale errors worthy of a Saturday morning cartoon. But no cartoons at our house. Early on Saturdays little Eric and I headed across the yard through the fence, climbed up the cribbing and looked at the mess I'd initiated with very little else than dreams.

Twelve rooms of shattered plaster, a hallway join more than six inches off kilter, 103 broken windows and that's just the cosmetic end of things. The building would also need to be plumbed and wired. No discussion of heating or cooling systems except for the potential benefits of windows that would close, if they had glass, and if the frames hung straight. Itching to get my hands onto it.

Time slipped by as the foundation guys missed work days.

They needed to set the house before the rains. God forbid if we had an earthquake. Oh well, not a time to worry about something that's an infrequent event in California.

The earthquake struck October 1, 1987— a sharp jolt, meaning epicenter close by. I looked out the French doors of my bungalow to watch our debt load jiggle up and down. It turns out that the crisscross stacked cribbing actually allows for flexibility, and the structure resettled.

Emergency crews appeared at the front door. I hadn't dialed anyone but our good friends from the Los Angeles Fire Department came by. They'd assumed that there would be a crew on-site under the house, and they came prepared to help in rescue efforts. The foundation guys late again, nowhere to be seen. When Mudd arrived, he said the freeway was choppy.

No shit.

We missed our November 1 deadline to set the building into the foundation.

"We'll be set down soon."

Any more delays and the entire project would be a bust. No way to complete the rehab in order to finance my way out of the balloon payment.

California's rainy season arrived. The trenches turned into big muddy ditches like something out of a war movie. Missing the critical juncture could easily send our pile of lumber sliding back down the hill. Clearly Mudd had no idea how to finish the foundation.

Me, too damn mad to even plan a murder.

# CHAPTER FOURTEEN

# SUICIDE IS MESSY

## FALL 1987

I'd had enough and couldn't find the way through the problems. Started planning my suicide over crap that wasn't even my fault.

Hanging? No that doesn't always work.

Shoot myself? Terrified of guns, and I'd never learned how to work one.

A razor in the bathtub? Nah. Eric would never take a bath again. Couldn't I just disappear? Like Tinkerbell?

Always the go to, barbiturates. Okay, drugs would be the way to go, but how, where and when? I couldn't just get them at Lucky Market. Nobody I knew even did drugs any more. Some hallucinogens made you think you entered a portal to death, especially if you took them during PMS. Bad trip. You woke up back in your own body.

Maybe an accident in the big house. Let's see, what did we have to work with? Great supply of broken glass, stinking of rat piss and decades of dirt. Filthy carpeting, perhaps a good infection, but that would take too long. A fall? Nope. Afraid of heights. Besides, I'm clumsy, would probably do it wrong. Broken plaster but couldn't think of how to use it to kill myself. Turned out I was wrong. Mineral dust sets up a really vicious form of pneumonia and I hadn't been wearing a respirator. Again, too slow.

Then there'd be the issue of my rather substantial remains.

Would it be easiest to die in the backyard and just fall into a hole? I didn't want Eric to find a mess. For one thing, the kid wanted his world neat and tidy. At four years old he knew the alphabet and demonstrated to me that you could use this really cool invention to organize things like your spice cabinets or record collection. Picked up his toys, organized his little shirts by color in his closet. Who was the mother of this little control freak?

Then I started through the pages of my appointment book. Lick finger, grab edge, push. Good grief. I had meetings, contractors, clients, rehearsals, and of course the night school classes I taught for extra cash. Dammit. Maybe Tuesday afternoon the 7th? I'd even call a sub to teach the night school class.

How in hell do people make a clean job of suicide? I didn't want any casualties other than me.

Days shortened. Our sales team brought down the largest accounts in the history of the industry, but ...dammit, why was I broke? Other than a mortgage, child-care, car payments that sort of thing? I tired of earning 59 cents on the dollar with men less capable or committed than me. Guys who reported to me earned more than I did.

After an eighteen-hour workday in Houston, my boss Alvin took me out for a midnight sandwich and beer. We'd worked and traveled together for four years, shared candid conversations after long, long workdays. My efforts to request equal treatment did not go well.

"Sure, women get paid less. What if your child catches a cold and you have to stay home?"

My child had been ill with scarlet fever and I brought him to the office with a sleeping bag. I brought him to the office on Saturdays when I packaged client bids, sent him back and forth to the trash can with single sheets of paper so that he was working too.

Alvin continued, "Single women, you know, they're less reliable in the work force. Married women get pregnant and miss work." That night I learned the difference between a mentor and an ally.

I was just plain tired, of work, of everything. Didn't feel like conversations, corporate backbiting and compromises. The company authorized a home PC because I could no longer open up the office in the middle of the night in order to make East Coast deadlines.

Breathe. Cooked real dinners again. After story time, Eric and I both snuggled in the king-sized bed, each of us afraid to spend the night alone. A Disney cartoon rolled through the VCR, light and color in the nighttime. After a weekend with Don, he had the whole thing all figured out.

"Daddy can marry Linda and I'll marry you!"

Oh my God. They're going to put us on TV or in jail.

I listened to my child breathing beside me, my eyes open, tearing up in the dark.

Fled to my work room to boot up the PC after midnight, a chance to build charts and spreadsheets to capture the work and expenses on the big house. Resolve a client project in the quiet before dawn. By sunrise I'd be ready to talk to the boss in Houston and confirm all my math. Weekdays Eric and I hit the tarmac before 7:00 a.m.

- Shower and curling iron – check
- Fresh suit from the dry–cleaning bag – check
- Concealer for bags under eyes – check
- Lipstick and earrings – ummm....
- Check pantyhose for snags and runs – good enough
- Heels – both shoes the same color

Wake child, dress him, and throw on an apron over the entire corporate get up, run through the kitchen for yogurt and granola, coffee. Feed Sushi and Ceviche, Eric's red and blue fighting fish. At some point I made the mistake of setting a potted plant and Christmas ornaments behind their tank. Thought the colors would complement the two fish, who bashed themselves into the glass wall, killed themselves trying to fight the ornaments. They floated to the top, eyes bulging open.

Out the door for another 10 hours.

# CHAPTER FIFTEEN

# SANTA CLAUSE
## DECEMBER 1987

Tinsel decorations slung all over light poles on Ventura Boulevard. Retail malls blared carols in synthesized Musak arrangements—not peaceful, not really holly jolly.

By midday Friday the offices where I worked quieted down. The confederation of long-fingernail ladies went to lunch, coiffed hair, no salad dressing on their silk blouses. Single, married, divorced, we shared our frustrations, held each other up by the back zipper when needed. Right now, I needed them. I'd had it with Don, didn't know what to do next. Everything I owned, everything I did, had his name on it.

"Look, the bastard jumped up from the couch on a Saturday night, said, "I've got to get to the ATM and make a deposit." He didn't get back home until after 2:00 a.m.."

The sales reps looked around, just not at me. Norma quipped, "Oh Connie, sounds like he made a deposit, but not to a bank. "

I spilled my drink.

Somehow that anecdote put us all in a banking mood. The biggest financial challenge lay ahead, putting my own property in *my* name. My former boss, Terry, had worked as a mortgage banker. She'd found my construction lender for me. Her brilliant red hair flashed in the sunlight.

"Connie, how's the big house coming?"

I showed her pictures of the house still sitting on cribbing, pieces of foundation underneath. "I'm hanging on by my VISA card. Fucking contractor's defaulted to his suppliers. They don't carry tequila."

Terry stared at me wide eyed, glanced back at the photos. "I thought you'd be a lot farther along than this. What you need is a rich man."

"Good grief, that's the last thing I need. Don would crawl out from under a rock to pull his money out of the bungalow. His name's on the big house too. His dad loaned us the money to buy the land."

How did I ever get stuck with all this responsibility? Go get my head examined, sure, but not today. On Fridays I had to turn in time sheets to the construction lender in order to draw funds to pay my workers. Another damn errand before afternoon sales meetings.

My new job? I actually didn't report to the women's team anymore, bit into a Houston promotion like a dog on a bone. I could count and talk at the same time. The guys recruited me into Federal contracts, enormous accounts that racked up tens of millions in revenue for the company. Ex-military men on the team knew the smoky rooms, but technical proposals had to be completed by deadlines, compliant to hundreds of rulings. This was the top of the food chain. John's new directions on my projects? "Here. I'm leaving this up to you. All I'd do is spill coffee all over the bid and jam the printer. You need to learn my signature." We chugged Maalox all day.

Life: Some assembly required.

John decided to mine for corporate gossip one evening. He bought the drinks. Me, always single malt scotch, water back.

"So, what do the California ladies talk about?" I must have been feeling a bit snappy. Women's lunches none of his business.

"They're all looking for rich husbands so they don't have to work anymore."

"That's funny."

"Why?" I gulped my water, slapped down the glass. Picked up the tumbler.

"Because you're the one most likely to meet someone." His green eyes looked straight through me, I avoided that look, stared into my drink, wished I'd ordered something that needed to be stirred. John cared.

"Oh yeah, I'm a real find all right." My hand didn't shake, but the whiskey rippled in my glass, set it down, folded my hands in my lap. "Why?"

"Because you have your own cash, and you work hard. Rich guys don't want to be trapped into the sugar daddy game anymore."

I had to laugh. The men in my team earned more than twice what I did, took care of their families.

"Right now? The only man I want in my life is a cute little five-year-old."

Flew home to my little boy. He'd stayed with his babysitter for three days straight watching commercials, hearing the babble of other little kids, kindergarten projects and the inevitable Holiday Show at school. Good Lord. An only child, Eric knew what a dual-income Santa looked like. Stacks of boxes with big toys, little toys, new clothes dropped down the chimney beside a big tree, covered in shiny Christmas ornaments and sparkly lights. He'd been such a good boy. That kind of Christmas would not happen this year. Two houses, car payments, daycare, took everything I earned.

We sat on the couch reading a story. I put my arm around him.

"Sweetie, you know about Santa Claus?"

A bright smile.

"Do you think Santa Claus does all that work by himself?"

Not a sad face but a very thoughtful one. "He has helpers?"

"That's right. Those elves do a lot of work for Santa Claus but they need lots of help from Mommies and Daddies."

"Oh." He held his two little Pound Puppies, this year's in group of stuffed animals. Looked down at them, patted each on the head.

"You're such a good boy, but mommy..." tears and mascara blurred my contact lenses. "Mommy doesn't have enough money for a big Christmas."

"Mommy?"

"Yes."

"Could you knit some sweaters for my pound puppies?"

"What color would you like?"

"Blue."


A couple days later a Christmas card from Houston arrived in the mail. In the envelope I pulled out a very large check from the Chairman of our parent company thanking me for my work that year. I'd known about executive bonuses, but never thought about who got them. I called John to thank him. He laughed, "Oh, I didn't have any input. Barney made the decisions. By the way, you're not to show up to the office until after the New Year. Take some time with your little boy."

Eric and I dressed up, went to see the Nutcracker downtown, front row seats.

# CHAPTER SIXTEEN

# DONNER AND BLITZEN

## DECEMBER 26, 1987

Day after Christmas, Eric returned from his stay with Don and Chuck, the piles of huge presents and restaurant meals. When he left a few days earlier he clutched the two little Pound Puppies in their new blue sweaters. I even knitted a heart into the pattern. My mom and I had more toys waiting for him, wood puzzles, new storybooks, Hot Wheels. He had enough.

Don offered to spend time helping me secure the old house against winter storms. I needed a second pair of hands to stand on ladders, get the openings covered with heavy duty plastic sheeting. I pulled on jeans and sweatshirt, applied lipstick, inserted contact lenses and, well, no blonde goes without mascara. I've got my pride.

Don and Eric held out a little box. Blue topaz earrings—actually very pretty. Eric's birthstone.

"They match your eyes."

Somehow that didn't make me feel any better. I knelt on the floor, took Eric in my arms, covered his face with kisses. Had plenty of Kleenex in my pocket. He and his grandmother began work on a puzzle.

Don and I stepped through the fence, climbed up the wet cribbing with our tools and the plastic sheets, heavy duty staple guns. Negotiated our way through the split front hallway to the first landing. Don and I set up the extension ladder and stapled plastic sheeting over the opening, battened it with pieces of lath. The sky threatened, black and cold.

Up six more steps to the nursery, that six-hundred square-foot room with closets big enough to hold bicycles, teddy bears, plus armies of tin soldiers. Long sliding drawers had room for blankets, nappies, and built-in counter tops some thirty inches wide. What a fabulous room for an art studio.

The filthy carpet stank of piss—a living monument to feral cats and teenagers who'd never been housebroken. Wind howled through broken window frames and along the wall that once held a hearth. The chimney wall gaped open, narrow bookshelves and a few loose bricks in what would become a cozy fireside reading corner.

Rain poured through the split in my house and we heard distant thunder. Don and I hurried to install heavy plastic sheeting over the eight-foot wide opening where the fireplace once stood. Wind gusted through the open wall, picked up plastic, pulled it from the roll and blew it like a jib sail. I grabbed the plastic and held it in place. Eventually we got the upstairs opening covered but, the wind told us, not sealed. Hands sore, we put down our staple guns.

Don's hand grazed my back, a familiar, but also strange touch. "It's clean over here." We settled on the banquette for a break. He slid his hand under my sweatshirt. I turned away, no idea how to respond. Somehow, I reacted as the wife who had known him for eight years. On the floor were our old sleeping bags, a memento of zip together camping trips, a clean soft surface for a child to play and nap while mom worked. Rain started, and the sky blackened, purple bruised clouds providing a little daylight.

I lay in Don's arms, covered in that storm. Don looked around the nursery, "If we stayed married, we would have had ten children."

Silence. I just wanted comfort, not Don's sentiments about

things never to be. His dad Chuck came from a family of ten in Crab Orchard, Kentucky, where cousins married. Not my dream.

Crack! A blast of lighting, thunder so loud that the house shook on the cribbing. No foundation to hold us in place. The old house sat on a new hilltop lot, steel I-beams under the house exposed, by far the largest target for miles around. We'd been struck. Ozone filled the air. Rain pelted us, as we clambered down the timbers, avoided the steel beam, ran into the bungalow living room where Eric clung to his grandmother.

The sheet plastic on the two sides of the house held. Rain poured through the roof, down through the center hallways and rooms. The foundation delays cost me everything. I stood in my warm bungalow living room. What was I thinking? Couldn't save this mess, and everything I had about to wash away.

My mother, usually a practical woman, kept calm through my tears. "Honey, that house is made of teak. They build boats out of teak."

The scary part lay ahead.

In a few days, Eric grew pale, warm, sweaty. A swelling on his neck so large that he had trouble breathing. My son's fever approached 104. New Year's Eve, planned for Disney movies and popcorn, maybe a drink for mommy. Instead, I called the pediatrician, bundled the little guy into a blanket, headed for Children's Hospital.

We went through triage in less than five minutes. Doctors and nurses poked and prodded the little boy on the gurney.

"Mrs. R., how long has he had this?"

"Had what?"

"This swelling? Little kids sometimes get these. We think it's a branchial cleft cyst."

"What's that?" Apparently, the branchial cleft's a gill-like opening that closes after birth, when the lungs begin to work. His hadn't closed. Instead it attracted irregular growth. More bad news followed, an elevated white blood cell count, infection.

I tried to call Don. No response. Over and over. I needed help, I needed decisions, and I needed insurance information.

Finally reached Eric's godmother, gave her some phone numbers. She called one of Don's girlfriends who insisted "Oh, he's not here." We gave up. Miss M. wasn't about to sacrifice her evening for a sick child.

At Children's Hospital I perched on a chair, arms clenched across my gut, sobbed into my hands until angry tears steamed up my glasses. The New Year arrived, and I knew now that Don's loving gestures five days earlier had no meaning. I'd fallen for that, needed him, paid for that bit of comfort.

Welcome to 1988, the year that looked like living hell.

# CHAPTER SEVENTEEN

# THE MAELSTROM

## JANUARY 1988

Eric swallowed his medicine, gagged, washed it down with juice. No Rose Parade this year, no roses either. We'd had a frightening night at Children's Hospital, Eric pale, sweating, plugged into an IV. Bright lights and masked adults hovered around us through the night, monitored his breathing through the obstructed throat, the cyst swollen to the size of a tangerine.

I worked my neck to one side, then the other, heard the crunch, felt the stiffness. Left a message on Don's machine early that morning: "Do not call me. I don't want to speak to you, I don't want your voice on my answering machine. Eric's too sick right now to see anyone." No good wishes for Don, for this new year I'd had it with his indifference.

Within days Eric bounced back, fever dropped. He lapped up homemade chicken soup. His Aunt Faye came by and brought a new puzzle. Eric chirped and ran off to his room to play with it. He'd be ready to return to kindergarten after winter break.

Faye brewed coffee, looked outside over the fence to the big house sitting on timbers. The winter storm had cleared, left concrete blocks and wet bags of sand sitting in piles everywhere. We'd missed our November deadline to set the house into the foundation. The clock ticked away on my three months to get a Temporary Certificate of Occupancy.

Faye spoke. "Damn Mudd, I had no idea he'd screw you up like this."

Mudd had done an acceptable job on her house. We had no idea that he didn't or couldn't read drawings or instructions. He bid the foundation on the cost of pouring cubic feet of concrete, didn't understand a damn thing about fitting a house and a foundation together.

"Faye, this isn't your fault. We both thought he'd do a better job."

Mudd built a complete foundation, sunk it into bedrock. Then I called the mover to plan the set-down, connect the house and foundation. Mudd's back wall was eighteen inches short. No way for that house and foundation to fit together.

"What the hell?"

"Dunno. Just a mistake."

His crew returned days later, stacked bricks and mortar on the outside to make a second wall and fill it with thinned cement. God only knows if that's code or not. The inspectors came out, climbed underneath, looked at the weep holes, the pipes, ran some water. We passed. Of course the place drains, it's full of holes.

There was more. Faye's eyes missed nothing. "So, what are you going to do about Don?" Ugh. He'd pretty much dropped overboard, no sign or sound of him. Why bring him up on a sunny day?

Don picked up Eric a month after that New Year's fiasco. "We'll be late Sunday night. Going to a Superbowl party."

"No problem, but Monday's a school day."

On Sunday night, Don and Eric came through the front door. Eric subdued, silent, went to his bedroom. Don's face had turned brilliant red, everything from the forehead to the open neck of his shirt, eyes unfocused. He was blind drunk, and he'd driven up from Redondo Beach like that. He needed to get out of my house before I said something. Instead, he walked over to my TV, turned it on, and began yelling about the Superbowl game.

Don never watched sports. His reaction to sports talk? "Wait a minute, is that the little round ball, the big round ball, or the one that looks like a missile?" Tonight, his jerky actions in front of my TV unnerved me, his rage building as the TV responded with confetti and static.

Before dawn I stood in the shower, dazed, scrubbed myself raw. What a mess. Welts and bruises came up everywhere, my arms, my neck, my shoulders. I'd cried for hours without making a sound, and I could barely get my contact lenses in. At last the sun rose, and the nightmare could cease.

Work, a way to get control of small stuff when the big problems became too much. Sat in my office, holding it together, a scarf barely covering the bruises. Would another layer of pancake makeup help? Early morning sun glared at my blank computer screen.

A male colleague walked in. This gentle older man and I had worked together for six years, traveled together, shared sandwiches and late-night beers. He knew my little boy. He started to discuss a project. Alvin took one look at me, turned his head away and began snipping at the leaves on an umbrella tree.

Alvin's voice shook as he asked what had happened. I couldn't speak. I wish I knew what happened. Sat staring at my home screen when the phone on my desk rang, "Connie, what's going on?" John. All he heard was sobbing. I couldn't hide from John. We had shared too many confidences over the years.

The two men conferred, and then John came back on the line.

"Alvin is driving you to the hospital, and you are pressing charges. As soon as you've done your paperwork, we're flying you and your son to Northern California to stay for a few days, work out of a different office."

Leave all this? What a great idea!

Within weeks, lawyers blasted each other with letters, figuring out how to split our assets for themselves. Don called.

"If they lock me up, you won't get child support, and I know you need the money." Not like him to plead. I didn't really care. All the bravado, gone. Not sure if money played on my mind right then.

"Look, I want you and the boy to have the house. I also promised I would take care of him until his eighteenth birthday." Not so easy to extricate yourself when you've committed to a project that cost every household penny earned, as well as Chuck's life savings. We agreed on terms, typed it up and copied both lawyers. Our property, our decision.

Daily I looked across the way into my dream house nightmare. I couldn't ignore it, couldn't move forward. Months passed.

One spring evening Don and I talked of better times, of being April newlyweds years ago, and of our son. A new pattern emerged, one where he would come over twice a week to see the boy. We'd finish a bottle of wine together and Don spent the night. I could go on the road for work. When Eric stayed with Don, we shared goodnight phone calls from hotels.

I ended up with a stray dog who wanted a warm bed and a bottle of booze at night. We'd committed years earlier to home and career, to raise Eric into a prince, complete with his wooden castle. Did my ability to provide make me into some big tit in the sky? One who apparently didn't know how to say, "That's enough."

On the road again, client conferences. Men have the oddest solutions to problems. Over dinner John suggested, "Hey, American Airlines pilots stay in this hotel. Why don't you hit the bar and get lucky tonight, work off some tension."

Let's see, a tight skirt, pantyhose and high heels slung on a barstool, half dark bar, some guy offers a sweet drink and tries to touch my hand. Creepy. I'd probably get arrested for assault.

Put on sweats, strode into the coffee shop, glaring lights, pink chairs, table, not a booth. Not so cozy. On the menu chocolate ice cream with hot fudge, Snickers bars, yeah, that'd do. Alone in Dallas for the night, face down in chocolate and whipped cream until I passed out.

Days later, another Houston meeting. The national VPs gathered for late night drinks at the chairman's house, knocked back shots of tequila and slices of watermelon around his kitchen island. Our host offered a large bonus, and everyone had to state how they would spend the money: Peter wanted a condo in Maui, Barbara wanted a huge diamond, Tom, a Porsche.

"Connie?..."

The new national accounts were generating a staggering $70 million in airline ticketing revenue.

"Well, I've got a hundred tons of scrap lumber sitting on a hillside in Los Angeles."

"Hey, as long as you're moving houses, why don't you just bring that thing to Texas?"

# CHAPTER EIGHTEEN

# SHIPWRECK
## MARCH 1988

At last we were ready to set the house down into the new foundation. Mudd would be out of my hair. The movers came out, that same yellow gold truck with a magician working all the hydraulics. Once again burly men climbed into position underneath the house as the floor joists lowered, inches at a time, onto the new foundation. A little above each of the timbers, they'd whistle, stop, and lift out the heavy logs one by one. The giant I-beams slid out from underneath, and my house sat on the new blocks. Almost.

What a wreck. Doors and window frames hung awry, flapped in spring breezes. I was able to climb inside. The quarter-sawn oak floor tilted something awful, like a saloon in a movie set. Wood grain hid under dirt that workers tracked in and out. The original masonry, so carefully designed and constructed, now sat as a pile of used brick somewhere in the canyon. Scavengers picked through it to build their rustic garden walls. I'd have to buy all new bricks to replace the fireplaces and chimneys.

Pipes bent and twisted underneath the floors, every bit of mechanical structure ruined. No water or power here. At least we wouldn't need to worry about electrical mishaps. Frayed wires ran throughout the house, knobs and tubes tumbling out of her ceilings and walls. Twisted, tangled, useless.

I asked Mac when the movers would be able to reassemble the

house. They cut it in two. Surely the contract included connecting the main joint between the halves. We'd started our summer with a whole house. You cut a house in half, you put it back together, right?

Mac responded, "Ma'am you're gonna need a carpenter to put this thing back together."

My budget and timeline completely missed this contingency.

Mac recommended a local company from the valley. After the foundation fiasco, I wanted carpenters who'd done a "move-on." Made the call, and the gentleman said he'd be by the next afternoon.

His shadow blocked the afternoon light in my 53 inch wide front door. This buffalo must weigh at least four-hundred pounds. He tramped through the hall, stepped on my dining room stairs, their carefully wrought curved risers intact. Snap! The long oak treads split down the center, a curved riser shattered. When he stepped on the dining room floor, it bounced then settled some two inches below the baseboard. Two more carpenters came out, took one look at the house, inside and out, said, "No!" with good reason.

Frantic, I called Otto, my engineer. The main hall, split, does not meet by nearly six inches. The two halves abut, off level. Why? Otto advises, "You really need to do something to get that thing level…" You'd think that an engineer would be the right person to solve that problem.

The City Building Inspector visits, announces: "Lady, you've got to get that fixed."

"What do I do?" Someone's made a major error, but no one knows what happened or how to correct the error. This old house and I have stood in the same whirlwind, barely survived the same storm. No input, no advice. How do we go forward?

My crazy work hours crossed five time zones. On a Friday afternoon I got home in time to spend an evening with my little guy, but first I pulled on jeans and boots, reached into the pantry cabinet for a hard hat and leather gloves. All visitors must pull on protective gear to go down the cellar ladder, including the little boy. No sneakers, no baseball caps, no bare hands.

My flashlight struck the sills of the foundation over and over, but all I found? Tiny critters who ran for their nests. Impenetrable cobwebs festooned the gateway to the underworld. Climbed over the low block wall supporting the big hallway, then crawled on hands and knees through moist soil and broken bits of wood and glass toward the front, where the sloped cellar narrowed into crawlspace. In some places the timbers appeared orderly, but several joists shattered during the move. A peek through smashed foundation revealed the afternoon sun, and piles of dirt. My house looked like a ruffian with missing teeth, punched out in a brawl. Went back outside.

That afternoon I stood alone, gazed at the line where wood joins concrete block. Walked around the house, stepped and stopped every few inches. Examined the dining room side, then the living room side, sitting at two different levels. Toward the back, pieces sat closer together, but not even. Pulled out a tape measure and a plumb line from my belt and stopped at the front door. Stepped back, stopped again. Moved to the other side of the front and stopped, stared at the opening, astonished.

The house movers sawed off the foundation sills on the left-hand side of the house, readying it for a new foundation. They left the old broken foundation sills and shims attached to the right side. Sonofabitch!

Ran to the bungalow to dial my phone. The engineer won't return this call now, it's nearly five o'clock on a Friday. He picks up. "Otto! I need you to come to the old house, right now! I've found what's wrong with the foundation."

Chattered on into his silence. "The movers left the foundation sills on the right side, but they removed them from the other half."

More silence, I heard the engineer's uneven breathing.

"Are you sure?"

"Well, that's what it looks like to me. I found a bunch of extra wood on the right side."

Tore out of my driveway to pick Eric up from childcare, dollar a minute if I'm late.

Fifteen minutes later Otto's car pulled down into the dirt slope. His first words, "Oh my God. You're right."

"Okay, so how do we fix this?"

"Connie, your house mover needs to fix this. It's all their mistake. Those foundation sills have to come off."

"How do we do that?"

"They'll lift the house, tear them off, then reset the house right."

"But the hallways still won't match."

"They'll slide it in with jacks. They can move the sections until the house can be put back together."

On Monday the mover arrives with the yellow truck, the one with all the dials and hoses. His crew knocks off the extra sills and drops my hallways into place, with only a half-inch seam running down the perfectly aligned center.

We still needed carpenters to reassemble this mess. One lucky bit of calendar happenstance. In spring the television studios go out on hiatus, and an old friend offered to lend me a hand. Jim, a studio carpenter, had a family of five to feed, and cash under the table helped. Television sets have to be sturdy enough to keep actors from getting injured, and over the years he'd puzzled out all sorts of wrecks.

Jim and I picked up a truckload of concrete foundation piers, straps, and timbers. Crawled underneath the house, hung plumb lines to make sure that the piers would fit at a ninety-degree angle into earth under the house. A little tilt less or more than vertical would rock the place like an old ship.

I'm tall and broad shouldered, but my ability to swing a sledge had nothing to do with that. A four-pound sledge is favorite instrument of destruction. Somehow, I'd kept my cool for more than a year, hiding the storms in my psyche. That day my shoulders and back torqued, then I'd slam a post into place. Jim measured, tested everything. Once we started hammering, he used a level along each post to confirm the angles with the plumb lines.

We'd bolt a post, then lift the next timber.

Hours later I leaned my sweating body into a post, smelled new wood, breathed hard, satisfied.

# CHAPTER NINETEEN

# MENTORS
## SPRING 1988

Someone in her right mind would have been terrified. Eric and I needed to be in the big house by August. I paid the entire mortgage on the bungalow, and loan payments were coming due on the big house in June. The house sat next to our bungalow, a heap of sticks and broken plaster. Also, no electricity or plumbing. One misstep, and both my father-in-law and I would be bankrupt.

"Mommy, there's an old man at the door."

Gene Grau, I never saw him without a flat cap, don't know if he had hair or was bald. Wire rimmed glasses circled twinkling brown eyes. I'd known Gene for some years already.

The big house had three broken bathrooms and a nada kitchen. Cold clean water was the first necessity, before we hooked up cheap temporary fixtures. Yikes! Just the copper piping to the sewer was going to run me $20K, before one fixture was purchased. Gene and I discussed the contract.

"Young lady, we really have to use copper. The galvanized junk won't hold up and you have a nice place there."

I couldn't argue. Grandfather had taught us that too often temporary solutions become permanent solutions. Still, I was hesitant to sign a check.

"I gotta ask, where's your husband? Haven't seen him around."

"Oh, he left us. He's gone to live in an apartment now."

Gene's eyes flashed, "Dumb bastard." He paused, apparently his comment was not finished. "How are you doing the contracting? Who's running this for you?"

"City Hall says that as a homeowner I can do it myself."

"Oh, for Christ's sake, we'll use my number for anything that needs inspections. It won't cost you anything but you have to do quality work. He really left you with a mess, didn't he?"

Through the spots on my glasses, I looked at a cluttered living room and my grubby child. Eric advised Gene, "My mommy has a big hammer!"

The general contractor problem was solved, but I really needed to get my hands into something. There's no real power in paper—not even checks and cash, invoices, bills. What can they really do with paper? But wood, glass, tile...bricks even... When you have a fistful of nails and a good hammer, you have some damn power.

I walked into Frank's Highland Park Glass, an old shop on the corner of Avenue 54. The faded sign and dusty trophies in the windows didn't look promising, but we needed to start somewhere. Maybe these folks would know something about the other old houses in Highland Park. Victorians and Craftsman homes ran from Figueroa Street to the arroyo. Elaborate windows stretched from basements to the gables, enhanced with wooden mullions, leaded glass, etched florals, so many beautiful ways to bring in light. No aluminum and plastic fakes here.

Behind the dusty trophies sat a lady with an adding machine, dyed auburn hair and sparkly glasses, trying to sort through the piles of handwritten invoices as well as bills.

"I need to learn how to set glass."

She hit a bell on her desk. Not sure how she found the bell under the yellowed papers. An elderly man came out from the garage space—concrete and grease, unpainted walls, sheet glass stacked on carpeted dollies. No truck, no shiny logos.

I carried one broken kitchen window under my arm, a simple piece with only two smaller panes. Actually, I remember that the kitchen window dimensions were 19 1/4 x 13 1/4, every single one. With the moldings, they came out to 18 x 12.

"Oh, we can do that for you."

"Well, actually I need to learn how. I have 103 of these, and if you can teach me how to set glass, I'll buy all the panes from you." Frank looked at me, amused. I planted my feet, gripped my window. Looked him in the eye.

I learned to putty windows at my grandfather's knee. In our old New York Victorians, every child had a job. Toddlers made putty worms, and big girls learned how to squeeze the putty into a frame with a knife. These windows daunted me though. These windows were different, fitted with narrow wooden strips of molding, precisely cut little pieces. How do you take it apart without breaking the whole thing? I was ready to learn how to cut glass.

"I'm restoring a big house up on Mt. Washington. I've worked on windows since I was a kid, but not this kind."

Frank pulled off his glasses, rubbed them on his shirt. Beckoned me into the "NO ENTRY" area of the workshop. In the center was a very large work height table, covered with carpet. "Let's see what we have here."

The gray carpeting, taped in several places, glittering here and there with ground glass. Frank's hands were broad, all muscle. Wrinkles, age spots, and veins stood out on the surface, along with several small white scars. His belly pressed into the edge of the table, and he leaned over my broken window.

He did not wear gloves to remove the broken glass. Instead, he picked up a putty knife and began to pry at the wood molding. I was terrified. It never occurred to me that we would have to replace all the wood in all those windows. Good Lord, 500 strips?

"Young lady, we'll pry the moldings off. Start in the center so that it lifts. Then pull out your brads, that's right, push your knife under the corner, and there, it pops right out." The old wood bent but did not break. It moved forward just enough to get the knife underneath. Once the first piece was out, the next three could be pulled out easily. Then he handed me a wire brush to clean the frame and remove the bits of broken glass and dirt.

"Pull the nails through the wood, heads and all. You never ever try to push the nail backward, it will split everything. The little holes can be reused with your new brads or filled in with a little wood putty."

By now the window was just a pile of sticks. The exterior frames needed to be checked for pests, rot, and just plain wear and tear. Once they were cleared, they were scrubbed and sanded until the lemony smell of Port Orford Cedar came through. The moldings were 80 years old, and one of them split. I looked up at Frank, gasping, "Oh no!"

"Oh yes, some of them will break, but we just cut new ones."

"...and save your sawdust. You mix it with wood glue to make your putty. That way you know you have a match."

For the past seven years I'd worn oval nails, neatly filed, and always in some glossy pastel. Tapered fingertips could fold nicely on a conference table, cook, or sew, maybe some painting. Hands could always be cleaned up by Monday mornings. This evening I pulled out the nail clipper and cut the manicure off. Got into my carton of tape, putty, brads, and the new miter box. Several taped sheets of glass lay to the side, cut and ready for the weekend.

Grandfather's motto came through. "Busy hands are happy hands."

# CHAPTER TWENTY

# WINDOWS
## SPRING 1988

As the sun struggled toward the horizon, gray earth sleep spun its invisible threads around the city. I stood alone on the hilltop, looking at my treasure, a dilapidated landmark and neighborhood eyesore. Went back into my bungalow to pack up what we'd need for the day. Eric and I squeezed though the fence and across the dirt path. I climbed the ladder first as the child handed up a duffel bag. Other little kids would be in front of cartoons with a bowl of sugary cereal.

Then up he came, a bit dazed but smiling in his overalls and a little red backpack. In the backpack was a peanut butter and jelly sandwich for breakfast, a cut apple and a thermos of warm cocoa. His sleeping bag and some pillows lay at the end of the narrow pantry, which was now our shop. Paint and putty covered an old radio, but strains of music began to fill the air. A thick electrical line ran from my bungalow into the old house pantry, through an empty window frame. My coffeemaker plugged into the power strip. We sat down in the long abandoned kitchen, ate our sandwiches on the sleeping bag. Eric settled in with his Legos and action figures, building away. I poured a second mug of French Roast and pulled the first frame from the pile.

Stacks of windows sat in the big hallway, numbers marked on the wood, inside frames, on bricks, on plaster. What does DR6 really mean? And why is DR6 written on a strip of masking tape, adhered to an open dining room windowsill? These handmade windows pre-dated the era of power tools. Each original piece fit in a certain way, and even though the measurements seemed the same, molding strips might or might not fit exactly. Dining room window DR6 might vary slightly from DR4. If K3 was the same size as BR12, what did it matter? Old houses settle, and these windows could open and close before the move. The challenge lay in refitting and hanging them after repairs. I had a new miter box and saw, but my own cuts...well, some were tighter than others. Sawteeth take a fraction of an inch off of every measurement, I need to cut on the other side of my lines. Sandpaper was the best tool for getting exact fittings.

Plywood covered kitchen and pantry counters. My workshop roomy and well lit, even with no power. I installed vises and clamps next to the dry sink. New glass panes stacked in cabinets, alongside bottled water and coffee thermoses.

My frame lay on the counter, readied for an attack on the dried and scabbed paint, hardened and cracked putty. At first, scraped gently to see what fell apart. Then dug harder into stubborn ridges and cracks, scouring everything down as the fresh wood appeared. Eric picks up a sand-block and cleans the frame and each of the twelve sticks that held the glass in a three-paned window. Next, he gets to play with wads of putty. He pinches it from the can, rolls it into a ball, then a log, chattering at his creation. I smiled, examined his long worm, "This was my first job with grandfather and the uncles, when I was a little boy."

"You weren't a little boy."

"Oh, right. But I did make putty worms, lots of them."

Picked up his worm on my putty knife, squeezed it into place, repeated the process until each corner is neatly pressed into the wood. Set the glass. Perfect. Set it aside, picked up the next frame.

"Sweetie, can you get these little bits of loose paint off the sticks?"

He sanded again, while I picked up the brads and began pushing the pieces of the window back together.

The new window smells different—aromas of fresh wood, pine cleanser and the oily putty. Everything's new, and old at the same time—another chance. A spritz of window cleaner, and we pack the pieces between old towels and cardboard sheets, label each stack of frames by the room.

By evening it's getting too dark to see in our pantry workshop. This Saturday we rebuilt four windows. Only ninety-nine to go. Let's see, at two days per weekend, four windows a day, it'll take until mid-July to seal the house. We carry one last frame across the path to work on our bungalow patio. Eric and I hum as we sand the last pieces, smile at each other as the orange sun drops beneath the edge of the hills.

It's time to order pizza.

# CHAPTER TWENTY-ONE

# BORN AGAIN VIRGINS

## MAY 1988

Every Saturday morning began with this same ritual of sheet glass, putty, and sticks. I pulled windows from the piles one at a time, pried apart the moldings, and cut the glass exactly an eighth of an inch smaller than the frame. Grind, drill, hack, yank. Hours later my jeans were stiff with putty and a few windows smelled of turpentine and freshly sanded wood. Cleaned up my tools, locked the chest and headed for a shower. Cocktail time.

Don and I had separated and filed for divorce, but sometime that spring, God only knows why, the two of us tried again, a couple nights a week. I began to unpack my head over the first drink. Faye, separated for five years, never filed her divorce paperwork.

Sunset threw a blush through Faye's living room. We stretched out on her two sofas. Her harp picked up the glow, bits of colors glinted on the wall, but no angels slept here. Faye sat up, sunlight lit up her frosted hair.

"You know what we need? A Cat Party!"

Cat parties replaced our grandmothers' gatherings of big hats and long gloves, tea and tiny sandwiches. We kept the silver.

"Let's get divorced! With black lace and dead flowers!"

Always the party designer, Faye engineered a reverse wedding shower. Recycled gifts, games, tacky lingerie. Time to gather the coven of old friends from our weddings and baby showers.

"I'm in."

Two weeks passed. Faye collected an impressive selection of flowers from every Beverly Hills party, wedding and funeral. Dead, rotten, dried, or wilted—candidates for beer pitchers. Same with the collection of friends, lawyers, accountants, artists, straight, gay but veterans of broken hearts. We looked good on the outside, but lipstick and earrings detracted from crow's feet and fading cheek bones. Designer suits held together droopy parts from childbirth and covered secret scars. A bunch of middle-aged ladies wondering what the hell would come next.

Chalo's Red Mill House seated thirty. Chalo acted as a friendly uncle to all the college girls. At 6:30 each evening he put out the sign, "Sorry, We're Open." Our place, a spot to go and cry in our beer or call out for pizza if Chalo didn't want to cook. Faye and I tacked up streamers of black lace and well-worn lingerie on the walls and curtain rods. He'd witnessed our pranks for twenty years.

A party of men came into the restaurant and Chalo warned them that he would be busy with a private party, sat them down in the back. They ordered beer. No hurry on their dinner. Lot of good-looking women coming in the door. Might be a fun evening.

Friends showed up in their least favorite boudoir outfits, expensive trash. I jammed my bits into a black lacy corset under a blue work shirt, a perfect pin-up for a hardware ad. The cuts on my hands hid under a massive bouquet, complete with yards and yards of frayed black ribbon. Not flowers you would want to catch at a wedding.

The men shifted their positions at the back table, looking over the collection of middle-aged women. Someone commented on my corset ribbons. "One yank and..."

Faye shouted, "You'd better leave her alone! She's into power tools these days."

Chalo stepped out of the kitchen with trays of flautas and soft tacos. A chunky friend reached into the platter of crunchy rolled tortillas filled with meat. She glared at the men through her thick glasses, bit down hard. Crema sauce spurted everywhere, ran down her chin, landed on her bosom. "Go girl! Bite it off!" Not sexy.

Loud stories of worst nights ever did not persuade the six men to leave. They watched us pull some tables together. Chalo stood by the kitchen door, and his glance warned them to stay back. The boudoir fashion show was under way. Faye's negligee sported white feathers. After all, she's a concert harpist. Diane, a CPA with gray hair and a killer body, showed up in a black leather corset and garters under her suit jacket. After four marriages and six kids, a shoo-in for the "Most Marriages award."

A voodoo doll appeared. "How did he hurt you?" Damn, you only got one pin. The little fabric doll, maybe five inches tall, came around the table. A pin in the cheatin' heart, pins in groping hands, the crotch. My turn. After Don left, I found Visa bills in the garage, fancy gifts of jewelry that I'd never seen. Month after month I'd covered all the household expenses because he came up short. Amelia drew a Visa Card on its ass. I pulled out my pin.

The Oscar's worthy parade continued. "Most Abusive relationship" went to a lesbian friend. "Nowhere Man" to an eleven-year relationship without a ring. Hand calligraphed "Born Again Virgins" certificates came around the table. JoAnn headed for Chalo's freezer and marched out with a frozen dick cake—strawberry and frozen yogurt, coconut covered snowballs. The ladies tore into it, licking frosting, slicing bits.

The men fled our little Bacchanalia.

Garlands of twinkle lights surrounded a display of wedding photos on the mantel. Chalo wouldn't let us light the fireplace, but he had some old chairs out by the restrooms. We needed to sober up anyway, and he helped us set a bonfire out back. The wedding pictures burned in under ten minutes.

*Abandoned house*

*A cold hearth*

*Family of owls*

*Excavating the Keyway*

*Under way*

*Move first half*

*Second half arrives*

# PART TWO

*Imagination is sympathy, illuminated by love and ballasted by brains.*

*Elbert Hubbard*

# CHAPTER TWENTY-TWO

# MAY DAY!

## MAY 1988

I'd failed, dead broke and hemorrhaging money that I didn't even have.

Our little life in the bungalow swallowed my entire paycheck, mortgage, childcare, a pizza out once a week. Each month I covered payments that had originally been paid by two salaries. For nearly three years everything I earned went to planning for the big house.

I couldn't sell the bungalow and move into the empty ruin next door. Meanwhile, a second set of house payments lay fifteen days off.

Foundation delays caused the fatal error. The six-month construction loan would end with a mandatory balloon payment, refinancing contingent on having a legally compliant residence in the big house. Two months were allocated for the foundation, but six months later frustration went to anger, and I held my tongue to get a drunken contractor out of my life. We hadn't begun work on the interior except windows and doors, things that could be removed for work.

Weekends of swinging hammers and cutting glass, followed by sixty-hour work weeks with heavy travel gave no peace. Physical exhaustion did not result in sleep. Meals on the road only caused stomach upsets, source unknown. My mind whirred away at projects as the body ground to sawdust.

I needed to admit my failure to a trusted friend, Eric Warren, a television art director and partner in crime since the beginning of college. Old far before his time, he'd shaken his head for years at my predicaments.

Warren and his wife lived in an Eagle Rock apartment, one bedroom plus a massive garage for collections of books, records and a BBQ grill that they hauled out every so often. Graphics and posters covered every surface, and Dr. Demento, our go-to radio program. On the ceiling a metal sign read, "HIGH." Yes indeed.

Our joint expertise? Decorating sets for plays, in my case creating masterpieces of fabric and staple guns, until the notable day that he announced: "I'm fucking tired of looking out of my kitchen window at that filthy brick wall across the alley." We hosed it down and painted a Watteau landscape with cloudy blue skies, soft silhouettes of trees, a feat of trompe l'oeil on someone else's wall. Don't know if they ever identified the vandals.

Warren noticed the house in the canyon before we were aware of it. We'd walked through that house side by side for three years now. He stood in the canyon with Andee and me when we filmed the house move. An expert in local architecture and community preservation, he needed to hear this from me before the bank got our house. It wasn't his problem. I just needed to crawl away from my personal disaster movie.

He leaned back in an old recliner. I hoped for his insight, or maybe a wisecrack to make the loss bearable. I had no vision for life after the death of our dream, from there the picture went dark.

"You know, I'm not sure I should mention this, but," he looked across at me, "I'm working with…Action Pictures…they're making sort of a "Ninja Western" and they, well, they need a ratty looking place for a hide-out."

Studios go on hiatus every spring, give artists a break to

generate new shows. Some actors vacation. Everyone else takes on independent projects, non-union, creative pieces. Warren worked pick-up films while Warner Bros. went out on hiatus.

"Can't promise you a decent flick, but their checks don't bounce. What's the chance you can get it cleaned up within a week? We'll even drywall it for you and pay you a couple grand."

"The thing is, this won't save your ass, but you'll get another month, maybe two, of time to hold off the banks."

Reprieve!? I hit the freeway, off for my evening Master Chorale rehearsal. For the first time in days I could actually see a road in front of me.

I'd kept up my place as a professional singer in Los Angeles, couldn't imagine life without music, hours of peace and reflection, time to breathe, to share voices with some of the best singers in the world, or at least that's what Zubin Mehta said about us. I studied scores on airplanes, warmed up my voice on commutes. Floated Eric Warren's idea by friends, Samela and Mark. Mark grew up building, said, "Let's put together a work party, like an old-fashioned barn raising."

Mid-evening break time, a few moments when people announced other concerts and opera performances, Mark stood up.

"Connie really needs help. We want every guy we can get to come by this Saturday with hammers." Several Los Angeles Master Chorale members knew of the caper by now. I followed up on Mark's plan with calls to friends and put on a pot of beans. The likelihood that people would come by to clean my house on a precious Saturday, not great.

By nine o'clock Saturday morning hammers and pry bars thumped and squawked against old plaster and lath. About twenty people appeared that weekend, tools in hand. Elaborate woodwork needed to be removed before the plaster could come down. We worked in teams, pried each piece from the wall, numbered and coded it by location. Energy and sweat poured from every corner. An old professor from Oxy stood on a ladder, opened up a broken ceiling, and pulled hundreds of nails out of old lath. By the end of the weekend we'd taken down the broken plaster from three rooms and catalogued all the precious woodwork.

Eric Warren's old van, the one we referred to as the "Can of Insanity," appeared in the dirt path. He had a flight of stairs in it, leftovers from a play, a sturdy construction that he thought might fit between the pantry door and the cellar floor. A couple extra two-by-tens to secure the bottom, and he and Mark installed the steps.

"Can't have an actor open the door and fall into the cellar. We've already taken out enough dead bodies."

Rooms stripped naked, bare lath, dust and dirt everywhere. We needed to prepare the three rooms for new drywall. The walls still rattled, some debris inside. When we tugged away at the bottom strips of rough wood, rat droppings poured down through the walls. Who knew that what people call the old house smell came from critters? Never thought about walls as a habitat. Raked and shoveled it up, removed fifty wheelbarrows full of rat shit. Just like that, she no longer smelled like an old house.

Meanwhile a drywall contractor came through taking measurements. The film company hired him, ordered a truckload of materials.

Warren took a look at the carpet, pulled up a corner. Rolled up the strips, took them outside. He looked at the first several feet. "You've got quarter-sawn oak floors, in beautiful condition." The carpet had protected the original wood. A producer looked over the room.

"Holy cow, you can roller skate in here! We'll be able to do dolly shots!"

Three days later a drywall crew got busy banging sheetrock into the studs. I picked up another roll of tape and closed seams. Cut, goop, spread. Loved the feel of the broad plaster trowel, smearing gooey compound, concealing the tape. Sponged it smooth, sanded the rough spots the next day. Way too preoccupied to think about July 1ˢᵗ coming or my cash trickle. I'd covered June.

Some of the repaired walls still buckled here and there, nothing straight in this old house. But the theatre folks brought laughter and energy. We started to paint, two days out from arrival of the camera trucks.

White paint? You kidding? Production Assistants hauled in a couple five-gallon drums of white. Curious. Designers never use white on a set, lights catch it and that's all you can see. The kids rolled in a first coat, moved fast. Warren mixed a second color, a soft ecru, the color of antique lace, grabbed a rag. He dunked the rag into the second color, squeezed it, and slapped the second color into the first. The two wet colors blended, smeared and feathered into each other, a soft finish adding texture to the entire living room. Four large paned windows looked up and into a bulldozed hillside, not yet a garden, and the beige reflected shadows that shouldn't exist. "Don't worry, we'll hang black fabric outside those windows. Nighttime."

Crew followed suit, rags dipped into the wet paints. Each hand splashed the two tones a little differently, heavier or lighter, streaky or spongy. The texture brought new walls to life, like grains in wood or stone. Shoulders and arms ached.

Good Grief! Already six p.m. and we had hours to go. Their location trucks were not anywhere near us, so I threw together chicken and salads for the ten or so who were left to work into the evening. Warren set up work lights for the crew. We ducked back through the fence in the twilight, plastered and painted until one in the morning. Hopefully the paint would dry for an eight a.m. load-in of the film. Three white rooms smelled of new plaster and window putty. New glass sparkled in a real house, ready for its cast and a pretend story about Ninjas, G-men, and the Old West.

# CHAPTER TWENTY-THREE

# ACTION, CAMERA, LIGHTS
## JUNE 1988

The crunch and whoosh of tires in the predawn came to a stop. Car doors slammed. Destiny knocked on my front door.

Everything hurt, stiff, sore and we weren't even talking about my battered heart. I'd worked with the film crew until after 1:00 a.m. getting a two-tone coat of paint over fresh drywall in the big house. Warren had contracted to repair three rooms and clean rubble to ready us for the final scenes of the shoot 'em up, slash 'em up movie. At 5:30 a.m. I felt like a final scene myself.

Staggered to the front door, opened it to a pair of bright eyes and a huge Irish grin, beaming out from underneath a ratty baseball cap. "Hi, I'm Chet, here to cook for the crew. Can you tell me where to hook up water and electricity?"

Peered at him, probably mumbled something like *"justaminute."* My little boy and I went to sleep in our painting clothes, mine a yellow T-shirt that said "WINCH," a play on words from my years as a RennFaire Wench. Dirty face, hair that needed a whip and a chair to get through any morning, let alone this one. Perfect.

I'd forgotten that film guys are cute, and I didn't date. Work, the old house, and little Eric had become my life. Ran for a washcloth, some clothes, opened the door again. Chet filled his 100 cup coffeemaker from the garden hose, and Maxwell House gurgled on a table in the back yard.

Shouts and mumbles rolled through the air. Crew members arrived at the long picnic table, griped about the crooked streets. They couldn't find parking. A PA ordered them to turn around, head back downhill to the Lucky Market parking lot, and carpool back up. They grabbed their paper cups of hot coffee and cold Danish, and trekked back up the street.

"Would you like some coffee?"

"No thank you." Sweet of him to ask.

A large white grip truck parked in front of the bungalow, cables strewn every which way through the neglected garden. Camera crews piled equipment, lights, and bits of scenery in the rooms. For this we had cleaned up fifty wheelbarrows of rat shit?

I stood on my porch with a china mug of French Roast. Another corporate upheaval was on my mind, and our team left to form a consulting group. Actually, not a bad thing. We had six month's severance pay as long as we didn't violate our non-disclosure agreements. Ah well.

People grouped all over the yard and lined up for my bathroom. It didn't really matter. The canyon outside my fence resembled an adventure tour to a remote location, accessible by walking through a gap cut in the chain links.

"Can I help?" Ready to join the buzz of activity, I dressed in a black denim skirt and yellow sweater, tailed by my little boy. Looked like the cook had a lot to do.

"No thank you, but your family's invited to eat with us any time we're shooting. Look little buddy..." Eric's enormous blue eyes, shadowed and sad, a shock of brilliant gold hair, tiny hands, thin. Instead of shooing him away, Chet steered him toward the table of Danish. "You can have anything you want." Eric sat down on an ice chest, licked the icing off the pastry and his fingers.

Packages of chicken breasts come out on the table, swiped

through the water in clean utility trays and laid on a large open grill. At ten in the morning, he's intent on some sixty pieces of pink meat, cooking them through but not burning anything. Pots of water boil on Coleman stoves, and sauté pans fill with butter, lemon, and cheap white wine.

"What are you making?"

"Chicken piccata."

The chicken breasts soaked in the fresh lemon sauce, asparagus steamed, rice cooked, oh... strawberry shortcake. Fresh berries, cakes and cans of whipped cream finish his presentation.

Fat girl meets chef. What could possibly go wrong?

By that afternoon all the neighborhood kids wandered around the bungalow yard, little fingers poked through our fence, peeked at the real live movie being made. Eric wore a baseball cap that belonged to one of the crew, and another crew member put a film vest on him. Chet arranged his red ice chests into a row by the fence so that Eric and the other little kids could have their own Universal Studios tram, narrated by real movie guys.

Our little bungalow filled up. My favorite Tante Sofia arrived from Amsterdam for her annual stay. Don came by for his Tuesday night visit. Early Wednesday morning he observed the film trucks, just laughed, something about "Connie's circus."

By noon I headed over to the barbeque where Chet slapped down burgers for fifty. A second man, looked like Bluto, was setting up buns and condiments.

"Do you guys need any help?"

"Nah, we're good. Doug, this is Connie, owner of the property."

"Pleased to meet you, ma'am." The bald biker with a good six inches of black beard looked me over.

I continued to talk to Chet. Something drew me into this sweet guy, a little slow of speech.

"Okay guys, let me know if you need anything. I'm home today." Then I babbled on, "Our office got cleaned out on Friday. Not even sure what I'm doing this week." Described my woes of corporate cannibalism to a couple of men who had clearly never set foot in an executive suite.

Chet's focus moved from the burgers directly into my eyes. "I don't really understand the problem. Don't you have enough with this house, your little boy? Your job is to save the home." He flipped the meat, slapped on cheese slices, and continued, "My mom saved our home, she continued to raise my little brothers after dad left. Sacrificed everything to make it happen."

Oh. Terrific insight, except but I didn't happen to have a half million dollars or the thirty-six hour days to make any of that into a reality.

That afternoon two crew members offered to move into the big house, rent free and help me put it back together. Nice, young, hardworking. Yeah, I could use a couple of set carpenters and an electrician. Maybe the time had come for *la vida loca*—didn't quite make sense for a mom, but hey, neither did moving a house.

Chet sat down on the steps beside me. "I hear some of the guys might move in here to help out. I could do that."

Oh Lord. "If a farmer fills his barn with grain, he gets mice. If he leaves it empty he gets actors." Some sort of quip on a picture at my grandmother's house.

Took a deep breath, pretty much flabbergasted. Would I be comfortable sharing a home with a hunk who just happened to live pretty much as a free spirit? Actually, wanted him to kiss me. Really bad idea. He went upstairs for something.

I mentioned all this to Warren, these guys hitting on me.

"I'd be careful if I were you." Good advice. I already had enough of a tangled mess on my plate. This didn't need meatballs.

Chet reappeared, no apron, jeans, or baseball cap. He was in a cheap suit, his curls oiled down, and a gun. A disembodied voice:

"Places."

"Quiet on the set."

"Action."

Chet and another guy dressed in a similar Goodwill suit storm into the open living room, in front of the enormous camera. Camera wheels around as more bad guys enter the scene. Who's a good guy? A bad guy? A funny rig had been set up in the dining room, wire and loops and a spring. An arrow shoots across the hall into an actor who is wearing a piece of plywood and a squib under his shirt. Ketchup and corn syrupall over the place.

A samurai type comes slashing through, Chet and his buddy fall, camera pans to legs and feet.

"And cut!"

Chet and the other actor jump up and give each other Dutch rubs. End scene.

When filming shut down that evening, the crew collected all their belongings. Eric returned his costume to owners of the vest and baseball cap.

Chet went down to his car and came back up the steps.

"Here, this is for your little boy." He held a *Bounty Hunter* cap, his previous film.

The car, a late model Chevy Grand Am, immaculate, with a USC bumper sticker in the rear window. Must belong to someone else.

"Oh, did you go to USC?"

Why did I open my mouth? Often people buy the stickers because they like football.

"Yeah, I did my MFA in Theatre there."

Did breathing stop, or did I take a deep breath? Can't remember. He drove off.

Next morning, I asked, "Did you give him the *Bounty Hunter* cap?"

"Sure, it's his."

"He slept in it."

Thursday's night shoot turned into a transformation. Heavy duty 100-foot extension cords ran from my bungalow into the old house. For the first time in many years, light shone through the windows. Mom, Tante Sofia and I opened a bottle of wine, thrilled to see a first glimmer of hope that something could come about right.

By dark the bungalow was jumping, a full sideshow to the filming next door. I couldn't flirt my way out of a paper bag, but this seventy-year-old Dutch lady knew how to charm. She poured wine for visitors, the grand European hostess.

"Cook, would you like some wine?"

Late that night Chet and I went for a walk. Stood at the guardrail and looked out at downtown lights and Dodger Stadium. He didn't try to take my hand. Fortunately I'd misread any idea that he'd be interested in me.

Oh well, I felt alive again. Took a long bath in my antique claw-footed tub, put on my favorite dark blue nightgown and slept like a baby for the first time in many, many months. Chet woke the bungalow when he arrived on Friday morning to hook up the kitchen.

He stopped and stared at my blue nightgown, "That's very nice, ....um... yeah, very, very nice."

# CHAPTER TWENTY-FOUR

# THE BOUNTY HUNTER
## JUNE 1988

Somehow our location manager blew it. Lost the location for the shoot. We had to move all our gear again. Wound up a bunch of streets in some LA neighborhood to the front door of a little bungalow. Where was the damn ranch? Knocked on the door of the bungalow; a sleepy woman and little kid blinked at me, like a pair of fuzzy owls.

"I'm here to cook for the film. Where's the ranch?"

"Oh, it's next door, but there's nothing there."

She led me to water and electricity.

Later that day I met another lady, a tall blonde in a business suit, a tall older lady, and one with a foreign accent. Little Eric trailed behind. The older ladies walked back and forth watching us all set up, took pictures of the darndest things—the grip truck, my open pit grill. No famous actors on this shoot, but they didn't seem to care.

Poured a cup of Folgers for the tall blonde that afternoon. She thanked me—didn't touch it. Only drinks French Roast. Apparently, she owns all this property, the bungalow and the big house, all this land. Damn. No wedding ring, but her husband came by on Tuesday. What the hell, he a traveling salesman or something? Kid wanted to show Daddy everything.

Her little boy and his friends are all over the place. His face and gold hair are like sunshine, happy, chirping and asking questions. I set up a tram with my red and white ice chests, one of the PAs narrates tours and movie stories to them. The guys lend them film vests and baseball caps to be "movie makers." At the end of the day, they take back baseball caps, tell the kids, "See you tomorrow."

Eric's little face, his happy mask, falls. So, on Wednesday, I go to my car and pull out one of my work caps, *Bounty Hunter*, a forgettable film. "Here little buddy, this is yours. You can have it to keep."

His mom? Tells him to thank me. We've talked a little. Apparently she's high maintenance. Needs a ton of cash and wants to get it herself. All upset about work.

My craft services guy, Doug, announces, "Hey, she's a real babe. You know, we could use a big place like this in LA for our bike gang. Help her out a little here and there."

She didn't look like a biker mama to me.

"She's got a body on her—look at those tits, that round ass."

"Um.."

"…but I thought I'd ask you, 'cause it looks to me like there's some sparks flying around."

"Nah. Go for it."

He did. She didn't.

The next day will be a night shoot—from noon until dawn. When I get to the house, Connie asks me, "Did you give him that hat?"

"Yeah, it's his."

"He slept in it."

We make magic whenever we put a story on film. That little kid needed a magic hat. Connie and I looked at each other for a minute, then I went to work. She began to clean her bungalow.

Yeah, we'd had forty people using her john, eating snacks on her deck. My trash cans sat in her driveway. She was really pissed about something, threw a toaster. It banged on the side and disappeared. Apparently, the blender was next if it didn't behave.

"You going to do that with me when I'm old and broken?" At 34 I had freckles and gray hair, a little thick in the middle. No serious lady since grad school. Pretty lonely sometimes.

"What?"

Silence.

The night shoot was magic. Connie sat with her mother and aunt, watching the big house. Lights were running inside, for the first time in years. The house teemed with energy, one scene after another lit in the dark—a ninja on the deck, an explosion, a final shooting with bow and arrow.

Meals were done, but I still had scenes to shoot. Actors gathered in her living room with bottles of wine and snacks that she'd bought. Her aunt held court, a gorgeous sophisticated European lady. Seventy? No way. A smile and a wink when aunt Sofia asked, "Cook, would you like a glass of wine?" At some point she suggested that Connie take me to the corner to see the lights from the city, spread out for miles.

I never touched her. Until I did. Kissed her in her hot tub. She raked her hand across my chest. Boom. I'd been on my feet for sixteen hours, she invited me to use her hot tub. Within a few minutes bathing suits and towels were scattered on the deck, and she suggested that her bed would be more comfortable.

Late next morning my biker buddy showed up with a truck to haul the barbeque away from her side yard. He knocked on her bungalow.

"Is Chet here?" I wandered out to her deck. Where did I put my shirt? Buttoned my jeans.

She stayed in bed. Her mother, son, and Tante Sofia breakfasted on the picnic table. Faye came by, packed them all into her Toyota for a trip to the farmer's market. An hour later the triumphal chariot returned. Tante Sofia carried a huge bouquet of flowers, all colors, arranged them in vases around the bungalow. Hearts and flowers everywhere. Maybe a bluebird.

So, I strolled across the back yard and into the front door of the old house. Sat surrounded by stacks of numbered pieces of wood, broken windows, discarded plaster and old pipes. Headed upstairs, first to the window bench where I'd sat, learned lines five days ago. The upstairs hallway a war zone, open to the sky. Rubble lay where they'd staged a pyro explosion Thursday night. That nursery wall had to come down anyway. The gangs already busted the lath and plaster, so the explosion saved her an afternoon with a crowbar.

I'm home, but she doesn't know that. I grew up in big old houses, just like she did. We can do this. Sat for a few moments on the library steps, where I spoke to her a few days ago about moving in to help. Wandered back outside, sat down on a log, and opened a pack of Camels. Connie looked out over her back fence and joined me on the log. Both of us in sunglasses. Can't believe I was going to pop the question after one night, but here goes. No big grin. Announced,

"I'm a one-woman man." Pulled off my sunglasses.

Motionless, she tries to catch her breath. Not successful. No air comes out, no speech either.

"So, what do you think about that?"

She gulps. Her ex-husband's never left the picture, has visited every Tuesday for the past year. On Thursdays he takes their little boy out for a deep-dish pizza. Finally, a response.

"I guess, I don't know, I've been out of the loop for so long. Why?"

"Because I'm thinking we both might give this a shot."

In her mind, silence and noise tumble together. Her brain reminds her that she has a home, a child, a big old house that needs a lot of work. She studies the dry grass. Was happiness even in the list of her desires?

She asked, "What do you see in this?"

I looked straight at her. She hadn't said no.

"I've never been able to resist the bird with a broken wing."

Don't care if it's proper or not for a woman to ask for help. She needs help. Period. But she's not about to give in. I've seen golden eagles fight, and this woman is tough, a skilled and effective predator, but willing to wrap a wing around her baby and pull it into soft breast feathers.

Her response to a gentleman's offer?

"And then what do you do? Break the other wing?"

Oops. Wrong metaphor.

She's a warrior, a woman with the ability to act on impulses and live with the consequences. She's also a stream of thought and actions, pouring love, anger, and money in all directions. A calm exterior masks turbulence bubbling under every surface, around every obstacle.

Me, I work on instinct and my instinct says, "Go!"

I stay on, cook dinner for the four of them.

Sunday morning, I go back to my apartment. Been gone three days. Need clean clothes, buy groceries, chores. Hardly been home in a month. My upstairs neighbor comes down.

Campbell snaps open a beer, "Hey buddy, haven't seen you in a while. I thought your shoot ended Friday."

"I've met her."

"Who, her?"

"Her. My lady. With the big house."

Campbell and I had been partying together for years. "Holy cow, you serious?"

"Damn right. This is serious as hell. I think she and I could make it work."

"Isn't she married? With a child?"

"Husband left a year ago. They're getting divorced. Little boy is adorable. Needs a dad."

Campbell shook his head.

"Good thing. You're Catholic. Can't have you hooking up with a married woman." He paused. "Damn, you're serious about this. Five years you've dated one nutbar after another. Gotta say, woman with a little kid and a big broken house kind of takes the cake."

Took Connie out for a lunch date a couple days later. She laughed about our whole improbable understanding. Wasn't sure she needed to add a boyfriend to her chaos, but then again, why not?

She'd gone to pick up little Eric after kindergarten the day before. Checked in with the teacher for a minute. At sharing time Eric announced: *They made a movie at my house, and my mom kept the cook!*

# CHAPTER TWENTY-FIVE

# ELECTRICITY
## SUMMER 1988

My washing machine stopped mid cycle. All the clocks stopped. Went to the junction box, pulled a switch. Nothing. Pulled another one. Nothing.

*Sonofabitch*! The film crew shorted out my electrical panel.

Money tight, I didn't need a new repair on my bungalow. Better call an electrician. My God, I'd blow all my film shoot cash and end up broke again. Chet out working on location, but it's not his problem anyway. For all I know, he'd got a new hook-up this week. Maybe he does this every shoot.

I called Ray, my electrician, who told me I'd need an extra $800 plus installation for a new box, 100 AMP power. Dammit. I should have had 200 AMP to run that film shoot. "Oh, it'll be OK. We're going to use a generator for the night shoots." they said. I looked at Ray, me, powerless, too upset to make decisions. Couldn't even make dinner for little Eric

Breathe. "Ray, maybe we can scavenge a panel from one of those abandoned buildings in the field."

He looked at me as if I'd been dropped from the moon.

"We just filmed in the old ranch house. The rest of the ranch is down in the canyon. Let's take a walk."

A puzzled look.

"There may be a power box on one of the old outbuildings.

There's a barn and stables, a caretaker's cottage down there. The cottage is in pretty good shape."

Ray understood one thing; he knew he was dealing with a madwoman today.

"Lady, if you can do that, I'll eat my shorts."

But he came along with me, if nothing else, to let me blow off steam and say *yes* to his bid. Also, I was paying him by the hour for the consultation.

Trampled grass and my giant sunflowers marked the paths down to the field, past the stables and the caretaker's cottage. No electrical panels visible. Stepped inside the old barn, found a box on the wall. Ray examined it, same make and model box as the one in the bungalow, this one, in excellent condition. We twisted at bolts covered with a generation of dried-up paint, unscrewed the box, carried my find back up the hill and installed it on the bungalow.

"Here goes nothing." Ray set the switches.

The washing machine went back on. Ray looked at me, shook his head. "Lady, this installation job? No charge."

Before the big house, I'd never been superstitious. Well, who's going to believe things we can't see? Sometimes logic fails. We go our own ways, leave it to the gods to sort out. In spite of my sense of responsibility and control over this process, I started hearing things. My grandfather's laughter in the field, the first sign. I felt the twinkle from his blue eyes, sparks flying around me when I undertook the hundreds of capers involved in the big house process.

Things began to right themselves. Normal for me meant going to work and coming home to my child. My former employers gave me six-months severance in the corporate shake up, set me free to accept consulting clients. A trusted friend, Jim, worked away on the rough carpentry in the old house.

Days into all this, Chet offered to take care of Eric because I had to drive to Twenty-Nine Palms for an early morning meeting. Two weeks earlier, Eric would have overnighted at Don's apartment. I said yes to Chet.

Left the house at four that morning, gorgeous drive through the desert, rose gold dawn, dark coffee and alone time. Worked on the Marine base all day, still able to count and draw up plans, enjoy a sunny drive back. Feeling clear headed for the first time in months.

Jim met me in the driveway, as soon as I closed my car door. A little anxious, what broke today? First words out of his mouth, "How well do you know that guy?"

"I've been seeing him a couple weeks."

"He moved all his stuff in here this afternoon."

Startled, I didn't know what to think. Sure enough, I found a set of weights, books, and an old handmade afghan in the front room. Eric bounced around with a baseball and mitt, Chet stood in the kitchen fixing dinner. I steeled myself, planned to sound gentle but firm.

"Um, what's this?"

"Hey, I went to the grocery store. Thought you'd be hungry after that drive."

A bright smile, he leaned toward me for a kiss.

"Oh my gosh, did I need something?"

"Well, when I got up to fix breakfast, all I found were granola and yogurt."

We ate yogurt and granola every morning, unless we had a PBJ all toasty and runny.

"So, I took him to the store. We bought eggs and bacon, and some Bisquick. I fried up the pound of bacon, ate two pieces, thought we'd have BLTs for lunch. Eric ate the entire pound of crispy bacon."

I'd been a vegetarian for eleven years, never cooked pork. Had never given Eric bacon. Chet stayed. That summer Eric gained fifteen pounds.

Eric told Don all about Chet, including the baseball and bacon. When Don dropped him off he asked, "Who's that, your new nanny?"

On my July birthday we packed up the neighbors' large SUV with eight of us and headed to the mountains. Our friends had three little boys. When Eric piled into the back with the other kids, three-year-old Brendan said, "Eric, is that your new daddy?" Eric looked confused. Don never went on picnics, but Chet? Chet had been running a picnic at our house for the last month.

"I don't know."

I panicked. Chet smiled.

When we arrived at the parking lot, their dad, David, strapped on a pack with one-year-old Brook. Chet lifted Brendan, set him on his shoulders. The two men strode up the hill with their burdens. Two moms followed, hands on the two older boys. We turned around, saw David and Chet already warming up with mitts and softballs.

My friend announced, "You can have the wedding in our back yard." Apparently, everyone except me knew that I should marry Chet.

On paper, Chet looked like a terrible choice for a husband. Low expectations, and who knows how he made payments on that nice car. If this got serious I had a lot of equity to lose. Late one night I asked, "Chet, how much do you make?"

He started one of his shaggy dog stories, hesitant, "Well, it depends on the film, they all contract me for different...."

"No. Chet, you filed a tax return last year. Tell me the number on the bottom line?"

"Oh, about $6,000-7,000 or so."

I made ten times what he did. At that moment, I only wanted his endless energy, some brawn, and that dazzling smile. Maybe a few kisses. Buried my nose in Chet's shoulder, slept, his smell bringing sweet safe dreams. Another day would reveal whether to grab him or run like hell.

We worked shoulder to shoulder in the hot summer days. Began to repair everything in the bungalow, years of deferred maintenance, getting it ready to sell. Chet had an astonishing mechanical talent and skill for puzzles with moving parts. My brother vetoed the idea of my escape from love.

"You kidding? Chet has more mechanical sense than the rest of us put together." A building engineer, Ron knew how everything worked. Mom, single for more than forty years, put her foot down. "I'm sorry, this isn't all about you. Your son's smitten, and I think it's mutual."

Like me, the house sat in the open air, its rear hallway hanging on twelve feet of cribbing. The front appeared level, but we'd need tons of dirt to fill in a driveway from the street. That would involve an expensive grading permit to fill a new slope, plus the cost of decomposed granite.

The grading contractor come up with an elegant proposal. He had to excavate a nearby project, a new home sitting on a flat pad. He needed to take down the hill on that property. Didn't want to pay hauling fees for twenty-five truckloads of dirt. Thank the gods again, the soils matched, and the city didn't need to know which piles of dirt went where. How about if he dumped that hill at my address, graded all that decomposed granite into a driveway for me?

In order to get dump-trucks of dirt to fill in a driveway, we had to get the steel guardrails and heavy wood posts removed. Chet soldiered out the front door in midsummer sun, pickaxe and sledge-hammer in hand, and singlehandedly ripped out every rail and post.

My mother sat on the sofa with a lemonade, "My God, he's a powerful and skilled worker."

Chet slammed into the dried soil, until he could loosen the posts at both ends of a rail. Then he tore at the bolts until they turned, removed the steel, formed neat piles of wood scrap and metal for someone to haul away. We now had street access, an actual address except for the twelve-foot drop from the edge of the asphalt down to our lot.

The dump trucks rolled in over the weekend, no inspectors afoot. Joe pulled up the dozer, pushed and smoothed the heap into an even grade, one that we could walk on or drive on up or down. Dust flew, and by the end of the day, we had a driveway.

The blades edged off a nice side slope, a perfect location for young fruit trees to hold the dirt. My birthday gift from Mom? An apricot tree in a whiskey barrel, ready to sink its roots into rich new soil.

# CHAPTER TWENTY-SIX

# THE SHOP
## AUGUST 1988

What on earth would make a woman dive into a mess like this? Connie's married to someone who doesn't love her. Her house is cut in half, torn apart board by board, a rubble heap comprises the rest. That adorable little boy works by her side.

They're one step ahead of disaster.

Gotta admire her grit, and her efforts. So far, a pile of windows and some new posts in the cellar to keep the entire thing from tumbling back down the hill. And why is her workshop in the kitchen? A power cord runs from the bungalow across the side yard and through a pantry window, along with a garden hose running through the kitchen. She stows saws, drills and sharp objects under the kitchen sink, safe and dry. Wow, doesn't she know how to cook?

The day I met her I was setting up breakfast and craft services in the kitchen, unfolded my tables and laid out coffee and donuts for the film crew. Bumped into a vise grip bolted into her kitchen counter. Warren, the art director for the film, dashed in fuming. "Live set! We've got cameras coming in and out of this room!"

Had to carry everything outside, set it up again. Okay, I banged into a few things, stomped around a little. Might have cussed.

Not sure what happened next, but I stayed. Never could resist a quest. As a boy, I lined up my knights for hours, planned battles. There's a lady to be won, or saved, or something, and the five-year-old is too little to take this on. They need a twinkle of hope, and a warm touch. I brought over my Grandma's afghan and my weights. I'm set, at least for the duration. A few days ago I almost went on one knee to ask her if I could give up my apartment and move in with her. Told her I'd continue to work in films and cook for crews, help her on my days off. Even supervise the workers she's hired so that she won't need to worry about the house when she's at work.

She seemed relieved, so here we are, but first things first.

There's a place for everything, and everything should be in its place. She doesn't quite get it. She's just dropped twenty grand on copper pipes. Yammers on about plumbing and bathtubs and such. She wants to scrub and paint stuff, make things nice.

This is not pretty. We head upstairs into her minefield.

An old bathroom stands at the top of the stairs, cracked mirrors exposed, a commode tipped sideways. Bent and broken pipes stick out every which way. The paper on its one standing wall peeled up in curls. Painted woodwork bubbles up like a psoriatic rash. Sheet rock and pails stacked against the wall. Connie sets Eric up with some toys in his room across the hall.

I grab our biggest crowbar, insert the long bar between cabinet and the one wall that's not smashed up, push down, yank the cabinet away. The woman looks me in the eye. We count: *one, two, three,* lift a six-foot bathroom cabinet, solid maple, steady our load on the stairs. At the mezzanine, we balance the burden on our boots, turn it, *one, two, three,* lift again. Damn. She can lift like a man. Says her grandfather taught her to use her arms and legs. Another stop to make the turn at the bottom of the stairs, and we carry the cabinet, step by steady step, outdoors.

"Eric, you can come down with us now!" Little feet thump down the stairs.

The kid grasps a man-sized scrub brush and a tub of Pine Sol, a pile of old washcloths on the plastic tarp. He's assigned to wash the old cabinets and shelves, get all that dust off, wipe dry with rags. Crazy. He already started learning to clean when he was three. Kid really goes in after the grime.

I've got a plan. Connie and I stand in this room behind the kitchen, examine the walls. Painters in 1909 covered the original plaster with canvas, then brushed on glue to prime the surface. Some canvas now peeled away, Connie has muslin and glue to cover the soft plaster. We move around with tape measures, babble on about dimensions. She's pissed about a huge burn hole in the floor where the little devils made a fire one cold night, nearly starting a canyon inferno.

Over and over we sweep and vacuum the back room, use Murphy's Oil soap, mops and brushes. Today it's the one room that smells like this house should: cedar and fir aromas, a taste of lemon. A new roll of wire mesh, spackle and caulk sit in the back closet. We study the holes bashed all the way through the lath. She cuts a patch, holds it, while I bang heavy U-shaped staples around the edges. Like an alchemist, Connie dumps plaster powder into a bowl, adds cold water. She slaps the caustic glob onto her trowel, too warm, burns bare hands. She pulls on rubber gloves while I position the ladders. I seal cracks with little metal disks, plaster anchors to hold the edges together. Plaster drips on our goggles as she smooths over the seams. Glop, plop, another drop falls on the floor. She bandages and tapes, like a nurse dressing wounds.

On Saturday morning we carry three buckets of warm water from the bungalow. Little Eric knows what to do, he's seen Mickey Mouse haul hundreds of pails. This back room, formerly servants' quarters, must be dust-free, sanded, wiped clean, primed, and finally painted.

"Little buddy, you never paint over dirt. The paint won't stick,

then you've got to buy more paint and do it all over again." I have
to teach him lessons his mom never learned. Look at her tools. Dull
blades, dirty hammers, plaster dust on power tools. "Plus, you have
to learn how to take care of your tools. WD-40 is our best friend."
Kid learns quickly.

While Eric washed the baseboards I brought in a heavy bundle
from the side yard, steel straps. The house mover pried out Simpson
straps when he pulled everything apart, but this afternoon I drilled
into every stud to set new straps.

"What're those for?" the boy asked.

"We get earthquakes here. We have to strap cabinets and shelves
into the walls, so they won't fall out."

"Like last year, when the house jiggled and mommy screamed?"

His mom comments, "We both remember that, don't we?"

Connie and I strap the bottoms of sturdy old bathroom cabinets
into the floor, bolt the bookcases onto the counters and fix the entire
structure to the wall. We set another cabinet crosswise, a wide one at
least twenty-four inches deep. Cover the burn. Hang padding in the
backroom closet and roll out more pads on the floor. Connie's stacked
and numbered windows now stand in order, initialed by rooms.

At last I install my peg boards and hooks on the free walls. If
the tool cuts, it goes in this section. If it hits things, you put it over
there. All the drills here. Woodworking here, metal working there.
We've bought plastic tubs, one for scrub brushes, another for plaster
tools, a locking bin for Connie's expensive power tools. Eric carries
tins of nails and screws.

*I've got a shop. Not quite sure why, but it looks like I've landed
this time.*

Grab my woman. Got her by the waist. Dammit, somebody's
knocking! No doorbell. We don't even have a door. A visitor steps
inside. Electrician? We don't need any more electricity today.

# CHAPTER TWENTY-SEVEN

# LIBRARY LOVE NEST
## AUGUST 1988

I love how the quarter-sawn oak floors catch sunlight, lustrous in brown and gold. Damp cloths pulled back and forth between the book and record shelves, erase years of gray dust in all the hard-to-reach places. The entire downstairs smells of Murphy's Oil Soap. We've been hard at work for days. The three of us take a lunch break at the bungalow. After our sandwiches, we stand in the side yard, examine the bungalow's chain-link fence. The time has come.

I pick up bolt cutters, snap the first links apart. Chet bends back the edges and removes an entire fence panel so we have easy access to bring what we need from the bungalow to spend a night in the big house. My boy scampers around with his red backpack, gathers up his toys to bring to his favorite room in the old house, the one at the top of the stairs. Chet and I have taken apart the guest room bed, antique iron bed, painted bright blue. Set it down at the side of the house. We get in and out of the house via a twelve-foot extension ladder to the kitchen door.

It's not possible to drag that blue iron bed up the ladder so we shuffle it around the house to the front door, set the head frame in the hallway. Foot railings follow, a full-size mattress, a couple pillows, a handmade quilt. My grandmother spent twenty-eight years stitching each hexagon by hand. So soft and comforting that I've kept that heirloom quilt my entire life.

Where should we put that bed? Three downstairs rooms have plaster and paint.

"Chet honey, what about the dining room? So pretty there with the vaulted ceiling, we could set the bed under the windows." The blue dining room, one of the rooms with no graffiti. Sunlight streams through the tall panes. I imagine a starry night painted onto that vault.

"Uh, Connie, do you have curtains for these windows?

Men and women just don't see the same things. I've landed at my castle in the clouds. I go for open spaces; he likes wooded nests. This is our home together, our tryst, a place to rest.

Chet looks around, takes my hand, leads me across the hall. "What about here, in the library?"

The oak library step, a memory of last summer's men and machines, the groans, bangs, blue-streak curses, all that whistling. In June I felt and looked like everything around me, broken and exhausted. Two days after we met, Chet sat down on this step, ready to solve problems, to work together.

My shock at his June assertion—I'd looked away, quite stunned. The young man, magnetic. Every part of me shrieked, "Danger!" Friends advised me *not to* get involved. Two months later Chet staked his claim, and here we stood, on that same step.

The library faces east across thirty-five acres of canyon, no houses, no neighbors. Its emptied windowsills offer a splendid view into the sunrise and the gorgeous Angeles Crest. Our new workshop contains stacks of windows heavy with new glass and putty, moldings painted in shiny black. We scan the pile for pieces LIB 1–2–3, pull out library windows from the stack. Workboxes hold the original hardware as well as shiny new brass screws. I shove a fistful of screws into my jeans pocket. Chet picks up a bucket of tools.

Somewhere under the house there are French doors to

complement the windows. I discovered these doors stored in the former basement downhill at the old address, netted in live and dead cobwebs but otherwise untouched. Here's a happy fact: Termites don't like teak. Someone had the sense to save those doors decades ago. Today plywood blocks the library doorway's light and air, shows spray-painted words: *No Trespassing*. Those doors will be a big improvement.

Eric runs back and forth to our bungalow, totes his favorite pillows and a stuffed toy, Marvin the Martian. By late afternoon the entire collection of Warner Brothers cartoon critters await him in his new room, ready for a little boy, maple planks washed, all loose wallpaper peeled and scraped away. Graffiti covers the light blue woodwork. Two sleeping bags folded together on the floor make a comfortable pad covered with his Tasmanian Devil bedspread, pillows on top. He's camping.

The night that I feared for months, deserting my little bungalow, becomes a celebration for all. Chet opens a bottle of wine and a packet of apple juice to dedicate the first painted and polished room. He pulls up the ladder, like the portcullis on a moat, except a bone-dry canyon serves as our moat. I stick a candle stub in the wine bottle, light it. All three of us snuggle on the little bed in the library. When Eric falls asleep, Chet carries him up the stairs to his new room.

Things are working out: the meals, the staggered work hours, the child-care time. Chet's locked into a new film. In order to make the long drives and prepare breakfast for a crew of sixty, he leaves in the dark hours. Each night Chet comes home with bags of food from his catering tables. Savory dinners of salmon, oriental vegetables and rice appear one night; lasagna with fresh salad, the next.

Eric thrives on our crazy schedule. The Kindergarten waif transforms into a rosy little boy who runs like a puppy behind Chet, carrying a hammer or a bucket of rags. He wears his own little tool belt, leather, like Mommy and Chet's.

Our all-night talks turn serious, conversations into the wee hours, both of us with dreams of what lies ahead. I want my lover but moving toward marriage terrifies me.

Chet's a thirty-four-year-old Irishman who wants the perfect bride. He goes over the mismatched items on his list. He calls this "ambivalent updates." He wants a Christian life and Christian wife. Oh, for heaven's sake, how hard should this be? I like Druids, Navajo sand paintings, any kind of candles, all the cool things that Unitarian kids study in Sunday School. I've toured cathedrals, memorized masses and litany in four languages, can sing the stories, the songs of the ages. As a singer I've spent more time in churches than he has. I'm not a Christian, yet he's with me.

This fellow hasn't been to church in years, fed up as an altar boy at the age of thirteen. The priests told him he should never kiss girls. Those fathers might as well have ordered him not to pick flowers.

He asks me, "Well, what do you believe?"

"I don't believe in believing stuff. I mean, it's like an echo. People go to church, someone talks, they repeat the echoes over and over."

We have a bed sitting in a pile of scrap lumber, and he wants to talk philosophy. "Hey, it's like you're a Catholic and I'm a vegetarian. What difference does it make?"

He rubs his face, hasn't shaved that day. "I'm not comfortable with your irreverence."

What makes him comfortable? I'm a good provider. He likes my hands. I stopped getting manicures last spring. I'm steady with a miter saw, cut strips of wood to fit a piece of glass, knead bread. He likes a generous heart. He's not sure about the agile mind, but I get things done.

I'm crazy about his mustached grin and the fact that nothing daunts him. When I'd hit the end of my rope, this guy appeared and said, "Why not? You just need some help."

But love? Unsettling. Wobbly.

Late into the night, we fold into each other's arms. Eric sleeps with his jumble of stuffed animals. Three hearts bind into one entity. The little one feels there's plenty of love to go around. Ah, the wisdom of innocence.

# CHAPTER TWENTY-EIGHT

# GRANDMOTHER ARRIVES

My mother came to celebrate her birthday in the house. Yes, there's cake, store-bought angel food with fresh berries and whipped cream. Grandmother visits relieved us from childcare. We were still moving in, and Doris played with Eric while we hauled everything from the bungalow, shoved furniture and boxes into broad hallways. She donated her comfortable sleeper sofa to the cause. It unfolded in the living room with an area rug and a Moroccan table, a camel saddle and a pair of embroidered leather cushions to complete our simple nomad set-up. She'd just come from spending three weeks in Spain and Morocco with an imagination full of adventures to share.

"Have you ever ridden a camel? The scariest part of the ride? When the camel gets up. You take your seat, think you're steady. They warn you to hold on, then the camel bucks, tips you straight forward so you face the ground, unfolds its front legs. The camel walks, you rock along, watch the landscape sway up and down at your sides."

Mom has a way of getting right to the point of any discussion. Everything we own sits in the stacked boxes. Chet leaves for work in the wee hours—coffee and biscuits in hand, the last batch I can bake before we disconnect my vintage O'Keefe and Merritt from the bungalow.

Hours later mom and I sit down to breakfast. The kitchen now holds a table and three chairs, as well as a good half dozen of Chet's red ice chests. Eric's emptied cereal bowl sits at his place. His Tonka truck worksite runs down the long hall. "Vroom, vroom! truck!" "Roar, rawr bulldozer!" Skip loader and rattling gravel pour from a dump truck while he reenacts his world.

"NO! You can't bring an actual scoop of dirt in the hall!" Right now I can't drop everything to play with him outside.

Mom takes a long look at me. "So, how's Chet?"

My coffee cup shakes a little. "Um, fine?"

"No, I mean, how are you and Chet doing?"

"I'm not sure, Mom. Maybe he'll want to leave."

"What?"

"I don't know what he wants. He's here with me and Eric, but—he might leave."

I actually had no idea what might be in Chet's head, or my own for that matter. What in fact were we building, besides a house?

"Might leave, or could leave?"

"Well, he's looking for a certain kind of wife, and I'm not his ideal."

Doris, a veteran of love and war; me a veteran of betrayal, loss, failure.

"Oh no you don't."

"Oh no I don't what?"

"You can't run this time. You've got to confront old wounds. They aren't Chet's problem."

Sniffles and tears. "I don't know. I don't know anything." Too true.

"Oh, for heaven's sake. The greatest mistake you can make in life is to fear you will make one. Also, I can't believe what you are saying."

Mom reached out, put her hand over mine. "It's also not like you. You know lots. What if he's looking at you, and looking at what he expected in a partner?"

"Well yeah, that's the part that doesn't match. It's like we match, but none of this was part of the plan. He's out shooting film, lives in his camping gear. God knows what I am these days."

Doris puffs out a deep breath, "What's wrong with Chet now?"

"Nothing's wrong. He's wonderful, but I'm, well, anxious. What if I mess up, or he changes his mind?" Clearly the wounds from a one-year separation from Don were not yet healed.

"Chet loves me, but he's looking for someone else. Mom, he's Catholic and he'd like someone never married and without a child."

Doris pours them both more coffee. With two children, she never remarried.

"What did you say or do?"

"I got mad. Said, 'Then what're you doing with me? With Eric? That's not going to happen. You think I can just shove Eric back in there?'"

"So, what does he say about your mouth?"

"He finds my cynicism disturbing."

"He'll learn."

Disturbing. Perfect. Is love ever enough? People seek love, overthrow their faith and discard their birthrights for this thing they call *love*. I know love, but I don't like failure. Mom asked, "So, why would you let past mistakes rule your future? And, Don wasn't even a mistake. You got Eric."

Doris looked across the table, down the hall to the Tonka truck worksite. "I'm sorry, but this isn't about you anymore."

"What?"

"All your issues? Not important. You love him, he's honest and maybe even loyal. Your son's crazy about him, and Eric needs a man in his life who's not Don. Get over yourself. Chet's built himself a shop right here. He's nuts about Eric. He's not going anywhere."

Our shop opened behind the kitchen. I owned a kit of tools, but Chet knew how to use them. New pegboards held a collection of woodworker's pieces, some handed from grandfather to Uncle Bill and then to us. Other tools exhibited their first coatings of oil and dust. Fingerprints on handles.

We're happiest when we work together. Passion, mistrust, emotional turmoil. What is this whirlwind of events. I'm not his type. He wants a little Irish wife? Maybe a pony too? On the other hand, he's thrown all his worldly goods, efforts, and heart into my journey with Eric and the house.

Deep, dark, rich love, an overwhelming comfort for all of us. Love writes all true poems, paints all pictures, sings all songs. It is enough.

The little bungalow next door went into escrow. All three of us, me, Chet, Eric, tool belts on, no turning back.

In thirty days, the tie line to the bungalow shut down. Others reside in the bungalow. Chet gave up his apartment. Our little family had no electricity. Without gas, no hot water, no laundry equipment, no stove. No more biscuits baked in the middle of the night.

Chet laughs out loud. "We're homesteaders. You need an axe and a well, we've got this covered." Set up his field kitchen in the side yard. No power? No problem. He'd spent a couple years camping on location, feeding crews on his Coleman equipment.

These mornings plumbers and electricians meet in empty rooms, examine bare studs and plan the routes for pipes and wires to twelve rooms. They've got to hurry. We're not habitable without a bath and a kitchen. Water runs, but electricity can't come on until every wire has been inspected and approved. Gas will take longer. Gas company won't look at us until we get a Certificate of Occupancy.

The treasures in our old kitchen survived a century. Cabinets, a full butler's pantry. Rock maple counters run under the kitchen cabinetry and throughout the pantry. A 1950s remodel to the kitchen included gray laminate around the sink and linoleum on the floor. There's hexagonal tile underneath hideous speckled linoleum. Kitschy wallpaper, with its flowers and teapots in gray and pink, now faded and filthy, peeled apart at the seams. I know the mind of that modern mid-century housewife. *"I'm willing to live in an old house with all that wood. You can have your dark study dear, but I must have my modern kitchen and bath."*

Thank goodness her mid-century modernization didn't include tile. Instead, buckets of white, or was it blue, paint adhere to the rock maple counters. Now it's dingy gray. Unlike other old paints, this stuff hadn't peeled at all. I fire up my favorite tool, the heat gun, run the heat gun, then a paint scraper across the countertops. The old paint blisters and peels, what remains dries into flakes. Masks on. Mommy loads her belt sander. Remaining paint crumbles away with the first pass of the sander, leaves gorgeous fresh maple, a few old knife scars.

Shelves are next. All our kitchen things sit in boxes in the laundry porch, glasses, dishes, canned food. Glass and wood cabinet doors lean against walls. Turns out little Eric's a tireless worker. My shoulders and arms ache from scrubbing away the grime. After I doff the gloves, an eagle-eyed little boy coaxes, "See mommy, look, you left some over here." He's right, a tiny speck of dirt escaped my eye. First a rinsing, then TSP—yes, phosphates may be bad, but damn, do they clean. Pine Sol, Murphy's, whatever we've got.

Cabinets and shelves wait for us. Eric's ready to use real paint, not finger paint, not kiddie paint that washes out of clothes. Grown up's paint. Chet shows the little boy how to use the primer. Fill your brush, then press it against the side of the can so there's only a little paint, feather it onto the wood, then dip again. Chet likes to work *dry*, no drips, no globs of anything left when he's touched brush to wood. I work a little drippy, wipe up a tiny spot. Scratch my nose, adjust the glasses, leave smear on my nose, fingerprint of white paint on the glasses. Eric follows Chet with his little brush, attends to each corner of the cleaned shelves. Turns out the kid's a natural.

A shout from upstairs, the plumber's men. They've run into a problem piping the upstairs bath.

Old houses sag, and two hillside moves have done their worst. The upstairs floor lies at an angle, slips off level by a few inches. Anyone with a spine knows what that feels like. They must correct the sagging before they can install the new pipes. The plumber examines the hallway ceiling and trudges his way to the upstairs bath. A few minutes later we hear him thumping his way down the creaking stairs to say, "We need some idiot with a sledgehammer to remove about six inches of concrete from that upstairs bathroom."

Chet's mustached grin, twinkling eyes, "I'll do that. Come on little buddy!" All afternoon Chet pounds and five-year-old Eric tosses concrete out the upstairs window. We have a deep ditch to fill where the dead-man posts stood. Rubble makes a terrific base.

Partnership means "not independent anymore," my greatest fear. Sometimes fear isn't practical. The house needs all three of us knuckleheads.

# CHAPTER TWENTY-NINE

# GHOST WORKERS

## FALL 1988

At times, the seam where they patched the two pieces of the house together groans, wood creaks, stair treads shift. Someone left foundation blocks stuck all over the place and the walls don't fit together right. Lord knows how the cement contractor got past building inspectors. They stuck a second block wall on the back when they realized that the foundation sat eighteen inches short of the back wall. Only God herself knows what will happen when it rains. The downslope wall will either fill up with debris and slide, or the double wall will provide extra support. Who knows?

A couple days later Chet goes away on a film shoot, somewhere in the desert. He's cooking over open fires in hundred-degree heat.

Clouds behind Angeles Crest turn black. A freak rainstorm hits, a real desert downpour in a hot afternoon. A river forms in the slick adobe under the house. A pop, then a gush. Why not? The main water line, a large pipe from the laundry room, begins to shoot water out the side of the house. The line probably had enough of the torqueing and creaking of the last month, the storm just a coincidence. I climb out the kitchen doorway, down the ladder, pipe wrench in hand, scan for the shut-off. However, the broken pipe exits a good eight feet in the air, on a slick clay hillside. No way to stabilize the ladder.

"Baby, can you come to the door? Mommy needs you to help."

Eric peeks out the opening, staring at the mud, the pouring rain and the gushing pipe. "Can you jump into Mommy's arms?" He jumps. By some miracle my feet and arms remain steady for him. He's about to do things he's never been allowed to do before. I've got to brace that ladder, slick adobe and all. Grab the ladder, sink the treads of my boots into the mud.

"Sweetie, remember the wrench in your toy set? The blue and yellow one that you put around the shapes?" I handed him the pipe wrench, a large and heavy version of the plastic one he'd played with since he toddled around in diapers. "I'll hold the ladder. You need to climb up there. Put the square part of this wrench around the pipe and turn it as hard as you can."

"Mommy, it doesn't turn."

Eric is on the top rung, tugging at the pipe, his pink cheeks puff and strain at the effort. "There you go. Good boy! Can you push it harder? Use all your weight." His toes still touch the ladder, but his full weight hangs off that wrench.

A sixty-pound child negotiates his first water shutoff. Late that night, Chet comes home to muddy clothes hanging in the laundry porch, hears the entire saga of the broken pipe. He Dutch-rubs Eric's blond head. The kid is now a full-fledged workman.

Speaking of rains, I can finally pay attention to the interior. The naked timbers took a tough, hard beating. The carpenter announces that the downstairs floor joists shattered during the move: "Ma'am, that's going to cost a lot for the 2x8s." First the foundation sills, now this. I turned my head, blinking away the dust, left the room. A long walk might help me figure this mess out. Headed downhill into the fields of dried wildflowers, took a little shelter in the cool barn, a great place to fuss and fret alone. Not even enough energy for panic and tears.

The barn stood empty, not even a bird or rat to stir the silence. I startled, felt the tap on the shoulder, heard my grandfather's whistle, the same sound that pierced the air as he called us kids to work projects. Rolled my neck, looked up at the ceiling, a ray of light pointing through the barn roof. Rafters, 2x8s. I received grandfather's message. Boots turned in the dust and I tore out of the barn, raced back up the hot dirt path to where Chet hammered shingles in place.

"Chet, Chet, come here!" He drops his hammer, looks for the emergency.

"Down in the old barn scavenging for tools. I heard my grandfather laugh, he tapped me on the shoulder. I felt him!" Grandfather's grave sits in an upstate New York cemetery. I stood there, wide eyed, sure of what I'd seen. Not afraid, telling Chet about it sounded, well, not like me. Chet looked straight into my eyes.

"I looked up where grandfather pointed, the barn roof, held up by 2x8s, straight, clear lumber. We can salvage them—every damn one!"

"You sure?"

"Well, I think so."

Chet yelled to his helper, "Campbell, we're going for a walk!" His sidekick dropped a hammer, joined us to tramp down the hill. The three of us examined the abandoned barn, sturdy post and beam construction, rafters every few feet.

"Well, shiver me timbers, let's scuttle this!" Campbell quips.

The men hauled ladders and pry bars, removed every third rafter by the end of the afternoon. Grandfather's laughter followed them back up the hill when they hauled salvaged barn lumber to the back yard, stacked the boards by the cellar opening.

Replacing the dining room floor joists still poses a problem. Clearly, no one can walk in the room until the new support system sits in place. The house needs to be lifted a third time to make this happen. An engineer is joining us for the day, to place our recycled lumber under this side of the house.

Downstairs, Chet and the engineer pull the five-ton bottle jacks out of a crate. The jacks don't weigh five tons; each one lifts five tons. This dining room takes four jacks, twenty tons of pressure. I hold the phone in case of, well, a problem,

The men insert the five-ton jacks under the subflooring. Chet counts off, everyone pumps the jack handles in rhythm. The sills must be vertical, plumb, ninety degrees to the ground. This would work fine if the house sat level on the earth. Instead, she's plopped in a lumpy bed of hillside clay, sandstone here and there. That's the problem. The salvaged joists and the dining room floor could smash into toothpicks.

The men confer. "Watch the whole thing for any type of movement." They pump, stop when a jack clicks at full load, stop, look again for any type of slippage.

Which way will the jack pop?

A yell: "Holy fuck!" Chet's language. His jack flies across the cellar, a projectile that can easily shatter a leg or fracture a skull. Note, no one goes in the cellar without a hard hat.

The men jump clear. Good thing. There are no spare parts for the men. There's always more wood and steel. Arms, legs and ribs, not so easy. Chet picks up the jack, reinserts it. "This motherfucker tried to kill us." Growls at the jack.

One more try, and they raised the dining room enough to jam new joists into place. After a long tense afternoon, the floor sat level, steel strapped for eternity.

The upstairs? I could rent out the upstairs rooms as a set for a horror movie, except that it breaks every safety standard in the book. A bisected hallway and bathroom, a cut through the bedroom. This afternoon I work alone on the demo. Chet's comment, "Throw away the Jane Fonda tapes. I've never seen a woman use a crowbar like that."

The nursery, largest room in the house, big enough to roller skate or ride a tricycle in, will also make a cozy upstairs apartment for the winter. Film crew did us a favor, saved hours of demo work by blowing up the wall for a pyro shoot. It's been an explosion scene since June. Plaster and debris everywhere, but no one touched the elegant joints. Even the vandals knew to bash up each other's graffiti walls but leave the woodwork alone.

Picked up my crowbar to finish the job. Pulled down the rest of the wall and broken lath. Ouch! "Bang, bang, bang."

A knock on the door frame, downstairs, out front. Squawking of the old doorbell. A strange man's voice calling, "Is anybody home?"

I pulled up my goggles, allowed the mask to settle around my neck, went downstairs crowbar in hand to cover any contingency. A face peers in, glasses, collar, plastic pocket protector. "Los Angeles County Tax Assessor ma'am." Oh, that's rich. "Do you know the owner?"

"I'm the owner."

"May I come in?"

He's well dressed, pressed slacks and shirt, shined shoes, proffers a business card. *County of Los Angeles Tax Assessor.*

"Watch out—I've got a lot of materials in here, this sheet plastic's slippery." He walked through the halls, heeded my advice about slippery plastic and dusty material, trudged upstairs to the half-demoed room.

"Um, ma'am, they've sent me out here to assess this property for taxes."

I can't believe this bad luck. All this work, and I get an extra tax bill? Not in my budget. The tax assessor looks down the broad hallway, lined with her lumber, cans, toolboxes.

"How about if I assess it as zero for now? You'll need to call me within the year to make a proper valuation."

The tax assessor confirmed the fact that this house had no value except in our dreams. I'd dissolved my assets into a hundred tons of scrap lumber.

# CHAPTER THIRTY

# INSPECT THIS
## OCTOBER 1988

Chet and I imagined lush views, polished hard wood, a warm hearth. None of that existed behind the movie set plaster in the living room and library.

We looked around our new realm. Turned out that I could paint, tile, repair plaster, scrape off wallpaper, band aids on a patient who needed open heart surgery. I knew only what lay *on* the surfaces of walls and floors. Chet knew building maintenance, how things work. The truth? Neither of us had any idea how to reassemble a really big, broken house.

The problems lay deep inside the structure. A giant Craftsman house sat planted in the hillside, severed into two pieces by chainsaws, cuts extending from cellar to roofline.

I'd already learned that general contractors don't take on capers like this. Why repair old houses when your entire livelihood is about building new ones? We'd moved into a five-thousand-piece jigsaw puzzle.

My new love tackled the job, me and my five-year-old. I agreed to hire a couple of his actor buddies, weekly contracts, decent wages. We needed studio muscle and know how, low budget guys who could make things happen on a dime. The rest we'd learn.

Here's what we knew how to do. We could hit things with hammers, cut wood and glass, pry stuff apart, and we could bend metal. The question: which do you do when? What happens when you break something important? Don't worry about that because everything's already broken.

Hitting things worked pretty well. We hauled bundles of steel Simpson straps inside, heavy metal band aids, holes in the edges to pound nails and connect studs. I visited a local forge to order custom corner plates, forged iron pieces that took two people to hold up and bolt into the corners of the long main hall.

The central axis of the house sat at the top of four steps that led to the nursery and to Eric's room. All off level, the stairs twisted like a Disney haunted house, a crazy mirror of parts that didn't match. Nothing could be joined, piped or plastered until the entire house lay straight, floors level and walls plumb. We pried off the stair treads to examine the space, set down old boards to use as a ramp. Eric loved the ramp outside his room, a great place to play with Hot Wheels. What in blazes torqued this stairway? Another trip to the cellar, flashlights on beams until we could see a slight twisting of the large pieces next to cellar stairs.

Stop. Call the engineer again.

"We need bigger hammers, bigger jacks and bigger bars!" Another team went under the house to adjust the center. Yes, lifting the house for the fourth time, to fix things that weren't balanced—once during the move, once for foundation sills, a third time for the dining room joists, and now this. Each time more lumber strained, more plaster cracked. This time everyone in the building felt the quake when the studs and braces settled into place. Lucky for us, none of the old lumber snapped.

Upstairs, drills screamed. Professionals worked getting wires run between open studs, piping into the kitchen, bath, sewer lines running outside. Chet and I cleaned, scraped and pounded. More hammers, more nails, more drywall.

September days suffocated everyone in the city, but breezes flowed through the open floor plans of our 1909 rooms. On the hottest nights, the old sleeping porch offered fresh air and a few stars above the lines of the mountains, late-night moments of peace after hours of sweaty labor.

Mornings brought the brain-bending struggles with city hall bureaucrats.

After a year of wrangling, City Hall couldn't agree on how to define land bought and paid for with a legal description a year ago. Don and I came up with the $60,000 cash, signed the deeds. A house now sat on the lot. Whatever. It's mine and I'm willing to squat.

What matters in "City Hell"? Infighting and grasps for power between departments. Cultural Heritage had one set of rules, Building and Safety something totally different.

The Parcel Map guys threw the book at me. Although we'd followed every instruction, they kept telling us we had a non-compliant project. The last parcel map in their files? A proposal for the abandoned DDW development. Because this rectangle of land once belonged to a developer, they levied some twenty-one conditions on my title. *Owner required to develop the land and structure as a new residence*, one matching eighty imaginary homes in a ten-year-old development proposal. *Owner to grade streets, install sidewalks and street lights*. The lists went on and on, requests from multiple agencies, a true municipal mess. Help! Dear gods in the heavens! Can't they agree on anything?

Neighborhood nuisance, eyesore, or curiosity? Pedestrians chatted with us. One day a gentleman came by with a yard sign, Tom La Bonge, a city council candidate. Offered him lemonade plus an earful of our problems. Yes, a yard sign would be fine. Happy to spray paint his name on the side of the house if he could help us untangle this mess.

Tom won the City Council election.

Days later a *klank* at the front door. We'd hung a small hammer on the door next a rusty old bell. Uh-oh. An important looking Building and Safety inspector appeared, clipboard in hand. Shiny black shoes, creased pants, a crisp white shirt, finally looked up at a clean-shaven face. Chet and I stood covered in shades of dust and plaster grout.

"Hello, I'm William Casillas, Senior Inspector. May I come in?" I opened the door a little wider into the dark hallway. "Oh yes, certainly." He took a couple steps inside, stopped.

"Oh my, look at this woodwork. Fabulous." He touched the hallway wainscoting, grasped the banister. Craftsmen feel for the grain.

"I used to restore houses." He started making notes. He didn't ask if we had a contractor. Thank heavens. Signatures on the permits named me as the General Contractor/Owner.

"You know, I came out of construction. Did a "move-on" myself some years ago. It's a big job."

Mr. Casillas walked into the living room where boxes of cleaned and partially wired fixtures lay on the inglenook benches. "Are those all original light fixtures? Wow!" He took a look at the living room chandelier, copper polished, rewired, rehung. "You don't have your electricity running yet, do you?"

"I've been on a tie line to the little bungalow over there, but escrow's about to close on it." He looked down at the floor, and out the window where a hundred-foot studio cord hooked up to the house next door.

Wrote on his papers. Looked across the living room. Film crew had screened off a ten-foot plywood opening where the original fireplace and brickwork warmed families for three generations. Missing, one wall, duly noted.

Our new Councilman had come through. He said he'd fix the Building and Safety end of things so that we could live in our prize. Mr. Casillas looked at the main joint, "I can see you've installed all your steel." Shining Simpson straps gleamed from cellar to rooftop.

Chet smiled at the comment. "Well, a lot of this is on the job training for me. I've worked on houses, roofs, barns, stables, but never a move-on."

I said, "So, what are your priorities?"

"First, you need to close up this floor. Run a board along to cover the split here in the hall. It's already securely tied, you can stain it to match."

"Any board, like a half-inch board along the cut?" Chet made a mental note to add that to the next lumberyard run.

"Yes, I'd go with six inches wide."

Mr. Casillas looked into the library, the little bed and wine bottles with candle stubs, a Tonka truck. "You don't have another place to live, do you?"

"Uh uh." We both shook our heads.

The inspector flipped some pages on his clipboard, the aluminum kind with the cover on it. Must have a good thirty reports already. "I see you've passed plumbing, but no gas."

No kidding. We took cold showers, and the stove sat there in the middle of the kitchen. Gas wouldn't come out until we were cleared for occupancy.

Chet asked, "How do we get power? We're about to unplug from her other house." An honest question. Held my breath.

Our inspector looked at us, glanced toward our work buckets. He'd seen Chet's tidy workshop. "Ok, this isn't exactly legal for living, but it's legal for you to work here. Let's get you set with a "Temporary Construction Pole" for power. You apply as a building site. I'll sign it with the utility." Of course. Builders need power to run their tools, lights for dark corners.

We walked back toward the living room. He looked at the plywood wall.

"So, have you guys ever visited the wrecking yards down on Soto Street?"

Uh oh. Will my house end up there if we fail our inspections?

Chet interrupted my nightmare.

"Soto near what?"

Funny, we'd driven over the LA interchange for years, had no idea what was underneath all those bridges.

"Olympic."

"They pull doors, windows, and cabinetry out of these old places all the time. If you're missing pieces, you'll want to get to know those salvage places." Mr. Casillas possessed a wealth of information for salvaging materials and rebuilding rooms in their original style. "I've seen really nice mantels down there, fireplace fronts, banisters. You'll discover pieces authentic to your time period."

Wow. That would be a dream come true.

"So, I could come out now and then, advise you on each step of the process, sort of a pre-inspection. If you follow the recommendations, we can clear you one step at a time. Also, you'll have to paint your exterior."

I spoke up. "Do I have to paint it before we even get these rooms livable?" Visions of empty cookie jars floated in front of me, no cash. "I'd hoped to do that in the spring."

He shook his head. "No. Get a coat of paint on the outside, the sooner, the better. That way no one will accuse you of a derelict house."

Good idea. Keep the neighbors happy. Also, paint would really protect our old beauty when the winter storms hit. Now to leverage the cash and double crews, one inside, the other outside.

Chet said, "I'm a good painter. We can do that."

My head spun—a glance at my boyfriend of three months, and a whirl of what I'd need to do to make this possible. How the fuck—how many actors does this guy know? We'll need the cast of the Ten Commandments to paint this house.

An hour later dust covered the inspector's spit-shined shoes, the sharp-pleated black slacks, too. The doctor paid us a house visit and our old lady passed a major check-up.

Power changed everything. Lines soon ran from our own pole into the house with multiple smaller lines taped down to the floors. Chet installed his hundred cup coffee maker on the kitchen counter, ready for duty. Hot tea when we wanted it, even a warm washcloth to take off my makeup.

Each night after supper the coffeepot hot water poured into the old sink to help us wash our dishes. We scrubbed and bleached every surface in the old kitchen. A hot plate and microwave sat on the living room inglenook bench, ready for Chet's movie set leftovers. No more ice chests. We plugged in the fridge. Only rule: one appliance at a time. Heat pulls a lot of juice.

Enough. We'd made a path to the initial rehab of the house. All quiet, we fell into our beds, sore muscles, plaster dust smiles and all.

# CHAPTER THIRTY-ONE

# PAINTING THE LADY
## OCTOBER 1988

Five-gallon buckets of brown stain sit at the end of the driveway. We're going to paint. The crumbling white paint isn't only an eyesore. The attempt at mid-century ranch instead of a quiet home looks all wrong. Originally, the house had dark brown shingles and off-white woodwork. Dr. Winter suggested shiny black accents on the window frames. I've dragged my feet on the color choice, never selected earth tones in my life. In New York, dark brown houses meant creepy, cranky old people inside. Pasadena's craftsman homes feature sunny porches, bright gardens welcoming visitors to big wood doors. After a talk with preservation experts, I understand a little more about the dark color choices. We can plant more sunflowers.

Scaffolding surrounds the walls of our old beauty, reminiscent of a lady's corset. Good thing fashions changed. Four of Chet's actor friends pound and clash, call for more steel, more heavy wooden planks. What in heaven's name comes next? The scaffold rises so they can replace shingles on the exterior, cover steel straps that mark the joint between the halves.

Chet and his actor buddy Campbell spend two weeks in the blazing sun, scraping away at older shingles, back-breaking work for them. They're both bronzed and freckled, Campbell's reddish hair turned brilliant blond with a sunburned bald spot. Like Chet, he's too old to try out for toothpaste commercials, and too young for character roles in films. His suntan and muscled arms remind us all of Popeye, Eric's hero. Chet's made the little boy a pipe from an old corncob and a chopstick. Eric's ready to work with the men. Well, shiver me timbers!

Any house is at its ugliest when all loose paint is scraped away. Everyone's arms hurt. We're down to bare wood, white flecks here and there, but deeper gouging would split shingles. Of course, this is the day when another one of those functionary inspectors shows up. Oh dear. Such a fine thread marks the line between failure and success. Hope he can tell the difference, understand our progress.

This inspector doesn't step inside. Instead, he paces around the house, examines the joints, pulls at old shingles. I take him to see the new siding on the back. Set into the lower slope, the back rises three stories, strapped all the way from the ground to the roof line, smells of fresh cedar, hundreds of new shingles hammered into place by two more actor friends of Chet.

Me, I hate climbing. I'm clumsy, afraid of heights. Huge extension ladders make me nervous. Rented scaffolds and staging platforms run up the back and sides. The peak over the sleeping porch stands some fifty feet above the ground. Truth is, I've never planned to get up on the roof.

Chet already stands on the top platform, calls out, "Hey, Campbell, come here!"

"Aye, aye Cap'n!"

Our motley crew ascends, steps out on the planks, waits for Chet's directions.

Chet hauled the paint compressor, machine the size of a large Hoover, up the stairs. Steps out the back bedroom onto a dilapidated sleeping porch, highest point of the house. They're going up to the eaves today. Scaffold stretches all around us, starting at either side of the top porch, fifty feet above the hillside.

Campbell clambers to the edge of the platform. Ladders and all kinds of power tools, cords, hoses, swing every which way off the scaffold. Campbell sits down on the staging planks. Clicks open a Coke and a Snickers bar for breakfast. Apparently, Popeye doesn't exist on spinach alone.

Chet calls out, "Hey, musclehead, a little early for drinking?"

"Soon's the sun's up o'er the yardarm!" Campbell sets down the Coke, jumps up to grab the other end of the compressor. Connects the heavy-duty cords, turns it on.

"Ahoy, cabin boy, come here!"

Eric runs up to the bedroom, starts to climb out over the railing to get on the platform.

Chet yells, "Stop! Throw us the line!"

Big eyes stare at the men, confused. I left specific instructions. Eric could not go out on the scaffold. He doesn't understand danger. We're talking about a tot who climbed to the roof of the bungalow at eighteen months. Chet points to the knotted cord, Eric hands it out the window.

Groan, whirr, the sound of air blowing through the compressor. Chet yells, "Blow me hearties, flow!" Paint appears at the end of the hose.

"When ya knows how, ya foist takes aim!" Campbell aims a spray of dark brown acrylic stain at the side of the house. Smooth, cool to the touch. Chet climbs out under the roofline, brushes Navajo White on the eaves. The cabin boy looks at the two men, remains behind the newly reinforced deck railing.

I've purchased a comprehensive Workmen's Comp policy for this troupe. Theatre folks create an entire world of illusion, but stairs have to be sturdy, lighting has to be safe, and everyone learns to use tools. Low budget films require an attitude of *I can make this work* and theatre folks know how to scavenge. All four fellows know their stuff. The June vision of film guys as workmen, now a reality.

Chet calls out. "Eric, go downstairs, bring us two of the empty work buckets, the big ones. Careful now—they don't weigh a lot but you gotta look where you're going."

Little feet thump down the steps, then bump, scrape, bump of the buckets he lugs back up. Campbell ties double knots on the bucket handles so they can't slip.

"Hey, don't do double knots! Once you've got the weight of the loaded buckets, you'll never be able to undo 'em." Chet picks up the rope, ties a slip knot with a safety. Rigs the pulley system for Eric to run things up and down, loading tools, paint, and, of course, jugs of cold water, into the pails.

Campbell ties off the rest of the knots. Years of work in theatre fly galleries and movie sets have taught these guys how to handle ropes. "Sure you want these safeties? Slip knot's easier to escape."

"Nope. I want things secure, no spills."

Best of friends, things have certainly changed. Chet's moved beyond a hot affair and a summer job. He grew up in a large and loving family, and the elements of that have dropped into his lap. He's still funny, but he's very serious about what he's taking on. Campbell, a confirmed bachelor with an MFA in Children's Theatre, has no plan to settle down to a job and a mortgage. Loves little kid's bright eyes and smiles, their moments of wonder. Winks and scrunches his face, "I'm Popeye the Sailor man!" Today they have to paint the house and entertain a five-year-old.

Popeye grumbles, "Oh my gorshk, that woman's got you tied up in reef knots! Good luck escaping those." Chet laughs, tosses the bucket over the side, lowers it to the ground.

"Hey! Cabin Boy—you there!"

Eric, fascinated by Chet's pulley system, loads in a gallon of the white paint and a clean brush. Looks up, "I lives in a garbage can. I'm strong to the finich 'cause I eats me spinach."

"Way, haul away!" Chet picks up the materials, climbs out under the eaves.

When I left for work this morning, I offered to take Eric to the babysitter. Chet said, "Nah, he'll be fine with us."

I warned, "Eric really gets into things. Here's the red leash from his toddler escapades. Use it if you have to." At lunchtime Chet harnesses Eric, allows him out on the planks for sandwiches and lemonade. No spinach for the boy.

Toot toot!

# CHAPTER THIRTY-TWO

# BEANS AND BLANKETS
## NOVEMBER 1988

Damn. These mornings were cold. Connie hid under the down comforter. I dashed for the kitchen to turn on the coffeepot. The house had cold water and electricity, but no gas. Sunny California sometimes reached eighty degrees in the afternoon, dropped to fifty overnight. Lot of good that did at the crack of dawn. We wore layers of sweaters over pajamas. She shuffled down the stairs, whimpering.

When the coffeemaker light blinked red, I poured some hot water into a big steel bowl and we washed our faces with warm washcloths. Through the service porch, a shower, also cold. Stiff laundry hung on lines. No dryer and who irons? Brush teeth in the laundry sink, check the face in a cheap round mirror strung up on the wall. Shave every week whether I want to or not.

The toaster worked. Fed the kid, we ran out the door. I drove Eric up to school, pulled three quarters out of my pocket for his lunch. In the afternoons I went for my jog up the hill and brought my little buddy home on foot. Little boys dawdle. No telling where he might end up on his own.

One afternoon Eric handed me a note that the teacher needed to see a parent. Strange. Eric adored school. Curious blue eyes and tousled blond hair looked up at the teacher, anxious to know things. Okay, I'll admit, I really didn't give a damn what I wore, and yes, my Tee shirts showed paint, dirt, and a hole here and there. No wonder Eric showed up to school with clothes covered in paint and plaster dust.

"Thank you for coming in, Mr. Hood." The teacher seemed polite and kind.

I waited to hear what Eric did in class, did he get in a fight? Not like him.

She cleared her throat. "Um, Mr. Hood, we have programs for families that cannot afford lunch."

"Nah, I give him lunch money every day. What's this all about?"

So, turns out Eric owed lunch money. He'd shown up at the school cafeteria for days without his three quarters. Each morning he would line up three shiny coins on the desk. Sometime after recess they disappeared. Oh crap. Connie had to deal with this one.

At dinner she asked Eric, "Sweetie, where's your change purse? The little red ladybug?"

Eric pulled the change purse out of his pocket, removed a small toy. Also in the pockets—tissues, a piece of candy, an action figure.

"Eric, this is important." The mother locked eyes with the son. "Your lunch money needs to stay in the change purse. Then you give the quarters to the lunch lady. Someone's been taking your lunch money."

The kid looked up, stunned. Why would someone do that? Connie didn't waste time getting mad or laying blame. "It's up to you to make sure you don't lose your lunch money."

On Friday night we sat at our kitchen table, enjoyed Connie's hotplate spaghetti and meatballs. She'd been paid, and her stack of bills lay ready for Saturday morning duty.

I announced, "We're going to Marshalls. Eric needs new shoes."

"Oh." A puzzled look, tired, bewildered. "Eric, go put on your clean socks."

She didn't say anything else. She knew my wardrobe came from Goodwill. I never, ever shopped.

Inside the store, she wandered toward the shoe section, ready to buy Eric a new pair of sneakers. I sat Eric on a stool, tugged shoes on growing feet. We selected sneakers, then little black leather dress shoes, no Velcro. "Buddy, it's time for you to wear shoes you have to tie."

Looked to me like Eric and Mom needed to start learning young man stuff. We continued through the store, selected school outfits, a dress-up sweater and corduroys. Connie dug into her purse at the register.

"No, I've got this."

Not sure what happened to my dream to play cowboys and cops in the movies. My agent sent me to audition for roles in films I wouldn't allow my grandmother to see. Silver kept showing up in my hair, and I'd eaten well this year. Casting directors and producers want current photos at all times. Saved up two bills from the work on the house, planned on new headshots. Thought maybe I didn't really need them.

On Saturdays elderly neighbors walked by our place to see our progress, sometimes told stories of the actors and singers who partied down at the ranch for years. Years ago a few got to glimpse Audie Murphy or Joel McCrea astride, exercising horses, or heard Sons of the Pioneers and others singing from the porches at John Ford's wrap parties.

In three decades the city had edged up to this canyon ranch, an authentic worksite, not a movie set. The outbuildings stood quiet now. Stables empty. The wrangler's house recently occupied, also empty. Mail poured through the slot for years after he'd left his knotty pine paneled home.

The barn remnants supplied the big house with needed lumber. We'd gone down two more times to salvage boards, removed alternate planks. One day no doubt I'd yell and push a wall, watch it tumble down. Evidence of the equines everywhere, rich loam from the horse manure would one day make a spectacular rose garden. Our biggest worry, fires. Fires had destroyed the canyon twice before.

Metal filing cabinets and a desk sat in the old barn. Shoved in among the letters, an old Los Angeles Times newspaper from August 2, 1957.

*Last night arson investigators were tracking down information that the fire was started on a hillside near Ave 37 and Roseview Ave. by two small boys. They said two witnesses reported seeing the boys dragging burning sticks through the thick brush along a hillside. Flames advanced into the ranch land.*

As a younger man, about in my twenties, I fought fires. Set the paper aside and took a good look at both sides of the canyon. Dry brush and brambles, eucalyptus, walnut trees. All of them oil based, drought resistant plants that would cause an inferno, even today.

*Firemen battling yesterday's disastrous blaze on Mt. Washington found themselves seriously hampered when a power line that supplies current to electric water pumps in the area burned down shortly after the fire started. A Department of Water and Power spokesman said pressure was partially restored to water mains by gasoline-driven pumps that were rushed to the scene.*

No way that worked very well. Holy Crap! Hope they've up-dated the water mains since then.

*Augusta Coviello, who was 17 at the time, was home alone when the fire started. She walked up to Killarney and spoke with a LAPD motor officer whose radio had died. He gave her several numbers and she made the calls to alert the city agencies of the fire.*

*She then went about rounding up five horses on the land, getting them to a corral where they would be safe. She suddenly realized that she was being surrounded by the rapidly moving blaze. One of the horses, named Trojan, appeared and came to her. With no time to mount the horse, she grabbed his tail and he led her out of the area just before the only escape closed behind them.*

*Los Angeles Times Aug 02, 1957*

Good Grief. We needed to have a talk about matches! Little Eric and his friends all turn six this month.

"What are we doing for Eric's birthday?" I asked an honest question.

Connie shook her head, "I don't know. Haven't thought about it—I can make a cake for a few kids."

"Campbell and I've been talking. How about we do a cowboy barbeque?"

Perfect. Campbell, me, a couple of middle-aged bachelors, ready to reenact our favorite 1950s birthdays. Why not? Eric should have a normal birthday bash. I've worn a Stetson my entire life. Mom actually kept my little buckskin jacket, handed it down to five little brothers. Bet that jacket would fit Eric. I'd call her to mail it to me.

Connie fusses. "Chet, how do you plan to invite twenty people for a party on a construction site? We don't have a stove, we have no heat."

"We can do it outside—barbeque and open campfire in the driveway. We've got twenty-five tons of raw dirt. We'll make a campsite! I'll clean up all the flammable stuff."

Connie's in. We hauled up my huge oil drum grill, planted it in the dirt. The woman must have a hundred recipes for beans. Soaked bags of beans, slow cooked them with a mess of spices. I bought tri-tip steak, hamburger and buns. Connie baked a chocolate cake. Campbell covered the beer with me. Also root beer for the little cowpokes.

"I'll show all the kids how to tie lariats and lasso. We need to get a bunch of new rope." She wrote down all my demands. "Where do you want the hangin' tree for a piñata?"

Connie scrunched her forehead. "I hate to put a ding into our new paint job, but how about we put in a hook over the back, where we're planning a deck? I'll hang a plant there later."

"OK, and can you make everyone a bandanna?" I wear bandannas every single day. Time for the kids to learn. She found her scissors and a bunch of cheap cloth.

Campbell appeared as the rodeo clown, nearly unrecognizable. Yosemite Sam? Or a dude from Nudies, the fancy dress joint in North Hollywood. Western shirt, boots, full make up, guitar and lingo for the little kids. The lariat and lasso stuff? Well, in a few minutes the boys all tied each other up. Pulled up the stakes and stabbed each other in fake swordfights. They took turns dying in the dirt. Except Natasha. Eric's fierce little girlfriend held all the bad guys at bay with her rubber band rifle. Raquel Welch, age six.

Campbell took over. "Ya little varmints, come 'ere and sit down." His lady friend pulled a pump out of her saddle bag, blew up the first long balloon, tied it. In less than a minute she had the first balloon horse, ready to ride the trail. Giddyap!

I had my oil drum BBQ going. The moms found a gallon of Paisano, some sliced up oranges and plastic cups. Connie brought out the pile of laundered drop cloths and beat up blankets. Also, some newspaper sit-upons, the kind every Girl Scout makes before the age of ten. The saloon was in place, complete with some mighty fancy women plopped on the ground, laughing at a bunch of foolishness.

Dads located the ice chest of beer, headed for the chuck wagon.

I rang my triangle. "Do you want a burger or a steak?"

Hungry folks, big and little crowded around. "Can we have one of each?" Ten pounds of meat disappeared along with the beans, bread, and beer. Candles and embers from the cookstove provided the only heat out there on that chilly November evening. Connie served chocolate cake. Six candles don't make a lot of light. Ate it with our fingers, in the dark.

The stereo, hooked up on the top balcony, played Sons of the Pioneers, a band that frequented this house a generation ago.

We'd all come home.

# CHAPTER THIRTY-THREE

# OWL'S NEST

## NOVEMBER 1988

I sat on a log in the canyon, gold leaves swirling in the breeze. Squirrels chattering, the clucking of a raven, a peaceful afternoon. The squirrels harvested black walnuts, or avocados when they could get them. One fat boy lumbered along a fence with an avocado in his mouth. My gaze shifted toward two old palm trees, decades of dried fronds hanging like hoary brooms. The palm trees marked the old driveway where our house had once stood.

Back to work. Chet and I decided to make the largest room in the house into a studio apartment. Old house drawings show nurseries for families with many children. This room had a fireplace, bookshelves on either side. Tin lined benches opened up, space for every kind of toy. Clothes closets and a walk-in closet large enough to make into a room on its own. Probably just the place to store bicycles, or for a nanny to exert a bit of discipline. Alcoves, shelves, and cabinetry hadn't budged an inch in eighty years and two house moves.

The 1909 woodwork, a joiner's masterpiece. Someone took days puzzling how to put this delightful space together. We never counted exactly, but the complex joints presented hundreds of corners to scour, dry brush, then cover with our fresh paint. For three entire days we painted the joints and frames to produce a lovely new living space, tan with cream colored woodwork. Piles of salvaged tile lay in boxes, ready to become a fireplace front.

The end of the long room promised warmth. Exposed stove-pipes and flues towered above the new firebox. I wonder what the birds thought about the frames and pipes rising above the house?

I'd soon find out.

Thumping in the hallway, Eric up and running around early in the morning, before sunrise? At sunrise? Who knows... my boy's an early riser.

"Mom! Chet! We've got an owl in the living room!"

"No there isn't. Go back to bed, Eric." Note: At this time of morning a normal little kid would be watching cartoons. We didn't have a TV hookup yet.

"No mom! I really see an owl downstairs."

Chet rolled over, sat up, reached for a sweatshirt. "OK buddy, let's take a look."

"Ugh." Chet once up, never came back to bed. I'd get up too, make coffee. Dug out my goose down bathrobe, Princess Frumpy, followed Eric downstairs. Sure enough, an owlet perched on the curtain rod. Question. How would we get him out of the living room and outside? Owls don't like the daytime.

We had an idea where he lived, probably in the attic that'd been open for more than a year. Dark, sheltered and full of mice, a perfect home for owls. We'd photographed fluffy owlets living in our rain gutters, probably hatched there. A friend once looked at the flightless balls of beaks and eyes, wisecracked, "My, I hope the children are getting enough to eat." Eventually owl parents stopped bringing mice and bugs and they had to flap their way out of the downspouts.

Chet opened a window. Owl eyes opened even wider, glared at us, but the owlet froze in place, terrified. The curtain rod felt a lot more secure than a windy roof or an open flue. We didn't want him to fly through the house, or crash into window panes and drop dead on the floor.

Chet set up guards in the space between living room and big hall, opened the French doors in the library, waved the fluttering the bird toward the light. Owls hate light, but eventually this baby moved his halfway feathered wings, flopped his way through an open window.

We concluded that we now lived in an owl's nest. Other people have cats to protect the house, keep it free of vermin. Our guardian, an owl.

We named our home Owl's Nest.

# CHAPTER THIRTY-FOUR

# A SURE FOOTING

## DECEMBER 1988

Old neighbors came by with stories of our home. As young men, some had even attended parties of the past. Cowboys roamed the canyon on their sleek well-fed, well-groomed horses. Gorgeous dark-haired women in long skirts and red lipstick laughed at the cowboy's stories. Over the years, cowboy actors from the 1960s turned into gangster actors speaking English, Japanese and Spanish, depending on the story. Bad guys and good guys took their marks on the sleeping porch, back lit, ready to confront pretend secret agents. Then they'd yell, run around and shoot blanks, except when they used knives or bows and arrows.

The presence of horses—old stables down by the barn, several feet of rich soil nourished by recycled alfalfa. Rusted farm equipment, plows and harrows, sat idle by unkempt orchards. Chet, raised on a ranch, explored every inch of the canyon.

Location scouts came in and out these past months, admired our broad open rooms, but their cameras chose the grubby passageways and empty window frames. Last summer a few short film shoots of our battered and peeling exterior kept us in much-needed building materials. Stock footage of my sunflowers paid for two week's groceries and gas. We need so much more. Weekly expenses for lumber and concrete dwarf the grocery budget. Little things like soap, gallons of Watco Oil and steel wool filled out the lists of supplies and tasks to complete.

Chet, along with his buddy Campbell, spent the summer hammering away on new shingles, replaced torn siding, repaired windowsills and trim. Ah, the fresh smell of new cedar. The smooth new paint job. Shining windows, all installed, await the coming winter.

All of us suffer from sore muscles and joints. My hot tub sits on gravel by the front door. There's no hot running water in the house, no gas lines.

This has to end. I'm tired of two-minute Navy showers in freezing water, hardly a dent in the bar of soap. Too exhausted to even scream when I run for a 50 degree bathroom. I wash my hair in a big steel bowl with water from the coffeemaker. The end of this is in sight. We'll plug in the hot tub as soon as the guys have a finished deck with enough outlets.

Engineering plans call for a new deck. For years the back walls wedged into a hillside. Now the front settles into the hill. In back the new cellar wall continues to the ground about eight feet below. The kitchen and library doors hang in the air, lead to nowhere.

This afternoon Chet and I hang a heavy-duty power line out the back door, swing it across the open space that will become a deck. We've lit the work area with 500 watt work lights placed inside the open doorways, blocked by boards and furniture.

"Don't touch these Eric. HOT!"

Our new deck must be strong enough to hold a 250-gallon hot tub and a group of rowdy revelers. The deck needs six large concrete piers, each sunk into a two-foot cube of concrete. The heavy blocks wait in their proper holes, ready for the concrete, dark clouds hover. Dammit. Looks like rain.

Piles of gravel and sand sit to the side, ready to mix into the barrel. I rented the equipment for the day and don't want to pay overtime, don't want to re-rent equipment again in a couple days. We study the sky, the volume of the raindrops. A real storm would ruin the entire job. Those piers must stay ninety degrees vertical. Dilute wet concrete, and we'll have pebbles plus a very messy redo. If we don't do it today, the sacks of cement will turn into boulders

Chet and Campbell stand duty over the cement mixer.

"Good grief, there's enough 'crete here to build a fort!"

The mixer tumbles and roars. Their battle cries erupt in the back yard. Next thing I know, the Civil War has erupted underneath my kitchen.

"We're gonna need it to hold back them rebels!"

Chet and Campbell face each other in battle formation, glare at the sky, weapons raised. Gen'rl Beauregard stands ready to pour the footings from his cement cannon. "Damn you Yankees!" they cry, and concrete comes pouring out of the mixer. A few cold drops of rain splatter.

"They're firing on Fort Sumter!" Gen'rl Anderson, played by Chet, stands by with the courage to defend his fort. A few more raindrops splatter over his shoulders. "I'm hit!"

Shovels ready, confront the pour, save the first concrete pier from the rebels as well as the errant raindrops.

Beauregard's shovel scoops more cement, sand and gravel into the mixer, but menacing clouds rumble again. From Beauregard: "Fire in the hole!!"

The concrete barrel whirrs. He readies another attack on the fortress.

"Cannon!" Anderson yells, "Men, take cover!" He throws a sheet of plastic over the wet concrete. Damp weather and mist will help the mixture cure into a solid block.

However, time marches on, faster and faster.

Upstairs looking out the citadel window, Maybelle with her

afternoon cup of tea watches, apron over blouse and suit skirt. "Keerful now! Gotta keep you two around to chop wood." She checks the darkening sky, switches on the work lights.

Anderson yells at his man, in this case six-year-old Eric, who doesn't quite know what the battle's about. He loves the yelling. The little boy stomps around in the mud, squealing like a pig. "Halt! Take cover." Anderson's shovel blocks the kid from getting any closer to the hole in the ground.

"Present Arms!" Anderson holds up his shovel. "Execute!"

Their cement cannon pours wet gray mix into the ditches where they've set the piers. Campbell scoops the concrete into the hole, smooths it along the edges. Yells.

From the cement mixer, "Return fire, sir?"

"Captain says hold yer fire. Need more ammunition. Use yer damn shovel!"

They scrape the remaining mix from the sides of the barrel, shovel in equal parts of the new mix. "Add water!" Eric comes a running with the garden hose.

The barrel whirrs again. Within the hour the two men filled six holes.

"Boy, come here!" Eric jumps up from the pile of building materials.

"Bring us tarps and them poles over there." Eric delights in his ability to lift and carry six-foot PVC pipes. A tent of tarps and poles will keep out the rain. Eric steadies the poles, the two men knot the ropes, swing the tarps into place.

I hang a white dish-towel out the kitchen window.

Campbell and Chet finish the pour, then surrender to cold showers and clean clothes.

'Soup's on!"

Sunny southern California rained for an entire week. A gaping hole in one side of the house measured eight-feet across and ten-feet high. The mason stopped by. Each day Bob said, "The firebox will be here soon." Some seventy years of handling bricks and boulders scarred the master mason's heavy hands. Nearing eighty, he apprenticed with Craftsman masonry under his father. Work boots scuffed down to steel, Bob's sharp eyes peered from under his cap.

Bob's sense of time, glacial. He's weeks behind schedule. Pencils, paper and phone messages disappeared into the ether around his impeccable aesthetic. He'd brought in a professional photographer, shot a portfolio of the exact placement of the original tapestry bricks, counted out each block, sourced the same type of brick for a solid wall.

Months later the bricks lay on pallets. Wind and rain blew against the flimsy plywood wall in the living room. A supposed warm hearth for a family became instead a blustery barrier, one with winds and dampness gusting through.

Overnight temperatures dropped into the forties.

I coughed and wheezed constantly, to the point where it was a distraction with clients. Phoned Bob early in the morning. "We really need to get going on this fireplace. We're freezing cold in here, no gas, no furnace. I'm afraid we'll all get sick."

"Oh, you'll need a carpenter to frame all this up while we wait on the fireboxes." Frame? As in wood? News to me. My old brick fireplace formed the side wall of the living room. The upstairs fireplace originally continued that brick wall, all the way to the roof. I thought that he'd get his fireboxes and then rebuild the old chimneys.

"Yep, your old chimney was solid brick, but nobody builds

them like that anymore. These days, builders purchase a prefabricated box of blocks and pipes to set inside a flexible wood frame. You need to meet earthquake safety standards. We'll do a brick cover on your downstairs firebox. It'll look the same. You can do the upstairs any way you want."

How *au courant*. Nobody in this house knew about the fireboxes. Bob continued,

"We run insulated pipes up through a wood frame, then build a stucco chimney over that."

Oh dear. I'd seen stucco chimneys on new houses. Never thought about it.

"But my neighbors have stone."

"You can cover the stucco with split stone, brick tiles, whatever you want, but that's all decorative."

"If it's prefab, how could it take longer than if you'd just had your guys here for a few days, laying brick?"

Bob comments, "Well, we ordered your fireboxes, but apparently the manufacturer must design and build them custom. They built these old fireplaces lots bigger."

How in blazes could they not know the size of the fireplace months ago when they counted out each brick? Since when is a fireplace oversized? It's just the right size to heat these broad beamed rooms. Same with the upstairs hearth in that expansive nursery.

"Your boxes'll arrive any day," Bob said.

"Wait, do you call the carpenters, or am I supposed to find someone?"

"Oh, I'll check in with them. Bye now."

I hope *someday* arrives before Hades freezes over.

Chet picked up the first head cold, then bronchitis. He continued to work, plastered the upstairs nursery. We bought an oil heater for Eric's room, kept his door shut against the construction dust.

Days later I lay out on the couch, cushions holding up my head and chest. The wracking cough is constant, exhausting. Can't even do phone work. Wrapped in comforters, a teapot and tissues by my side. Seize up once more, flecks of blood gather in the tissues soon. Pale and sweaty, I've barely got the energy to battle Chet when he threatens to take me to ER. Don holds the insurance cards and he can't know how sick I've gotten. He and his lawyer girlfriend keep threatening us, warning of a custody battle if we can't keep warm and dry. Eric has warm jammies and a down comforter on his bed. Okay—he's not enjoying the cold showers either.

Chet yanks off the blankets, tugs me from the couch. We leave for a few hours, return with nebulizers and bottles of pills. The phone rings. Dr. Who from Huntington Hospital. My chest X-Ray shows some sort of fungus all over the lungs, a viral growth, pneumonia. Somehow I sucked in plaster and mold right through masks and bandannas.

The first medical bills arrive, forcing a call to Don about the insurance and hospital bill.

The ex-husband tirade began. "What do you think you're trying to prove? You have no money, you're sick and my kid looks like a beggar..." Ah, he forgot to mention all they owed to Chuck. Don's father invested his entire life savings in this mess.

"Goddammit Don, I don't have time for your crap. Right now, I have to worry about a burned-out circular saw."

I slammed the phone in its cradle, yanked it out of the kitchen wall. Good sign. Strong enough to break things again.

Something scurried across the back steps at night while we all slept, too big for a mouse or a coyote. In the morning, when Chet opened the door, a brand-new circular saw sat on the threshold. Don went to Sears that night, drove thirty miles to deliver it. Merry Christmas.

Days later, Sunday morning light poked through the trees, a promise. Two young men driving an old truck pulled up on the street, nail-guns in hand. They attacked the pile of lumber, erected a frame and closed the living room wall. Headed upstairs, closed the nursery wall, framed a new chimney.

For the first time in two years, Owl's Nest boasts four walls. She is sealed against the elements and critters. Chet heated a little wine on the hotplate, something to celebrate. A few cloves, a cinnamon stick. The wine warmed our throats, soothed my chest. Soup simmered in a crockpot. Hot cocoa for the little boy.

Crockpots, crackpots, what merry friends we be.

# CHAPTER THIRTY-FIVE

# SANTA'S LITTLE HELPERS
## CHRISTMAS 1988

Christmas was coming. My VISA account looked like I owned a building yard.

This wouldn't be a big Christmas, we'd already discussed it. There was nothing more to buy, steal, beg or charge. My mom couldn't wait to celebrate our progress, and we had plenty of candle stubs and wine.

Chet shook his head when I jumped out of bed and disappeared into the closets that Saturday morning. I brought out a used shopping bag and a beat-up moving box—tinsel and all kinds of Christmas balls.

"What are we doing with that?" Chet asks.

I pulled out a staple gun from the work bucket, smiled. A glittering roll of used garland. Click-clack the staples and tinsel punched into the new fireplace frame. Handed the box of shiny colored ornaments to Eric who hung the first ones. Must be imagining things, the house seemed ticklish, no, shivering. How many years since someone had decorated her?

The custom fireboxes arrived three days later. We called Bob, begged him to make time to actually install them. He showed up, took a look at our pale faces, the three of us looking like victims of a siege. Outside, the mailbox clacked shut. In it a Christmas card from Chet's grandparents, a gift of twenty dollars for Chet, spending money of his own. He and Eric jumped in the car, ran to Baker's Hardware to seek the perfect axe and wedge, returned all smiles.

Eric and Chet ran for logs. Winter fuel wouldn't cost a cent. The fire department and owners of the thirty-five-acre parcel permitted us to carry off the deadfall from the walnut trees, dense oily wood that provided good heat. Illegal to chop them down, helpful to harvest anything off the ground. After running and carrying a few branches, Eric showed Chet his sled, a toy for playing in snow. They stacked a full load on Eric's plastic sled, dragged it toward the front door, ready for sparks, flares of matches, flames and embers.

Chet stood a fat log on end, raised the axe overhead, slammed it into the wood, buried the axe head, set the iron wedge into the crack. The wood split after a couple blows with a sledgehammer. Within the hour fire sparked and crackled before us.

Chet poured coffee, sat me down. A serious expression, but a gentle smile. We'd already talked all weekend.

He announced, "Eric needs a puppy."

"What?"

Eric and I'd already had pets, a cockatiel, an African Grey Parrot, the suicidal fighting fish, and the unfortunate bunny. Wildlife included a feral cat, a couple aggressive raccoons, and of course the family of owls. The canyon housed a pack of coyotes and every reptile known to California.

"A little friend of his very own, for him to take care of. He loves other kids and animals, why not?"

I munched on my lips.

By now we'd set up all the large furniture in the nursery, king sized bed, reading chairs, even a TV for Chet to watch football.

Eric's bedroom across the hall, a quick scamper after family time. All this surrounded by the war zone, immense hallways, a two-story stairwell and three bedrooms in need of plaster and paint. Gee, what could a puppy possibly add to all that? Chewing everything in sight? Peeing on new sheetrock? Puppy bombs to step in?

A trip to the pound to select a little black puppy, "Zwartepiet" the Dutch name for Santa's Little Helper. Chet visited his old apartment building with the new puppy, asked Campbell to hide it until Christmas Eve.

We scheduled a Christmas party for all the friends who'd helped us over the year. So many people made this dream possible. My mom treated us to a Restoration Hardware catalog bonanza, new kitchen lights. We painted the drywall a sunny yellow. Our electrician came by to install the new light fixture over the kitchen table.

"Where does this go?"

Dammit, what happened to the electrical box, the open wires? Oh, for heaven's sake, day laborers hammered drywall right over it. "Wait, I saw it, right here." I picked up the claw hammer, slammed the claw through the new yellow wall to reveal the box. The electrician gasped, certain I'd gone mad. White cabinets and brass lights brightened the cold kitchen, no stove, no gas yet. Empty hot water tank sitting back in what looked like an old kitchen chimney.

"Let's paint the dining room too!" We began the day before the party. The walls, not too hard, gorgeous teal blue. The vaulted ceiling? Oh, my lord, it arched over us, nearly three times the surface area of the walls. No way to sand this down in twenty-four hours. We'd roll on a coat of latex and deal with the ceiling later. One of those temporary solutions that become long-term solutions. Moved in the table and chairs, set up wine bottle candlesticks.

The evening arrived, along with pouring rains. Would people brave the trip to our dark hillside?

I filled the coffeepot full of cheap red wine, made trays of sandwiches. My personal specialty? Popcorn balls with peanuts and brightly colored candied fruit mixed in, pineapple, orange and citron, a few raisins and those weird waxy green and red cherries. Cinnamon, oranges and mulled wine warmed us before we could even find the paper cups. Friends brought trays of cookies, more bottles.

Campbell arrived with the puppy, dashed upstairs to hide him in the nursery. Twenty-four hours to go until the great reveal to our little guy. We shared the secret with Don, who picked Eric up for an outing.

The house filled with guests. Our fireplace roared, and a bearded man sat down at my newly refinished piano, squinted in the dark at song books and played carols. Singers perched in the inglenook, on the couch. Others lay against the embroidered Moroccan cushions, looked into the fire. Candle flames reflected glittering tinsel and ornaments strung on our fireplace frame.

Chet picked up a broken chair, an ugly old piece with molded carving. Snapped the legs off with his bare hands, and tossed them in.

"You're not going to burn that!"

"If it fits in the fireplace, I'm going to burn it."

The storm continued, rainy, windy and cold.

"So, Connie, what kind of drainage system do you have?" Our dear friend Stan, a civil engineer, began his career as a hydrologist. Stan knew how to put two and two together. He'd already noted the open ditch filled with gravel, because we'd placed lumber bridges across our cinder block doorsteps.

"Oh, we've got weep holes through the block walls, you know, half inch spaces with no mortar." Me, ready to explain the existing drainage through the cellar. No doubt diagrams would be needed to justify my explanation.

"You're going to slide right back down the hill unless we put in a system."

What the hell? The foundation contractor should have put in a drainage system? Not the one in the cellar, but a system of pipes to divert water before it ever entered the cellar? Dammit.

It's just plain rude to ask your guests to figure out your problems.

"Stan, I don't want to go out in the dark and look for drains. Have some more wine."

"I'll be over in the morning."

A pile of dishes waited when I got up. Up to my elbows in suds when Stan showed up in the rain with his teenage kids, Valerie and John. "Oh, Lord. You don't need to do this today. For heaven's sake, it's Christmas Eve."

"They need a good upper body workout."

"It's raining."

"They run in the rain. Look, here's your problem. If we don't get a proper drainage system in here, your foundation footings will fail. We've got to divert this water and we have to do it now."

"Look, I've got to get Chet to the ER." I paused, exhausted, "Stan, this really isn't a good idea today."

Chet planed the shop door just before the party. It wouldn't shut. He wanted to keep guests out. No reason to have a friend get punctured, stabbed, or worse. A huge splinter flew straight into his eye. No, I don't know why Chet didn't wear his goggles. We thought we'd gotten the damn thing out; we hadn't.

Stan and his kids shoveled mud all day.

Before dawn on Christmas morning, Eric burst through the nursery door, ready to jump into our bed. The puppy charged out underneath the springs, yipped. Eric squealed, and the two took off running in different directions, terrified of each other. Chet rescued the puppy, a little black ball of fur and piss, and ran after Eric.

"Buddy, this is for you!"

Eric put out his arms, held the little black lab, and they sat down on the floor, two little guys licking each other's faces. Zwartepiet joined our merry band.

Meanwhile, Eric asked Santa for a "knowing things book." First graders brim with limitless curiosity. Santa located *The Big Book of What Do You want to Know?* Nearly a thousand pages, loaded with drawings about volcanoes, bears and machines. *The Way Things Work* by David MacAulay, even more interesting. The illustrations tell about the insides of practically everything with moving parts.

Everyone got wool socks, work gloves. A small box from the Southwest Museum appeared, silver earrings with feathers. A minor infraction of the rules, but I forgave my sweetheart.

Months later, Stan's *temporary* drainage system passed permanent inspection. The three-foot deep trench required two layers of PVC and a Rube Goldberg of elbows and drains before a firehose stream of mud shot through the pipes toward the canyon.

Merry Christmas and bottoms up!

*103 broken windows*

*Born again virgins*

*Action Pictures arrives*

*Chet's shop*

*Eric learns about chores*

*Dining in style*

*Exterior*

# PART THREE

*I love you because you love what I love.*

*Elbert Hubbard*

# CHAPTER THIRTY-SIX

# NEW YEAR, NEW LEAF

## JANUARY 1989

Every damn ax blow vibrates up through my arms, into my back. We're in over our heads. Two hours every afternoon just to chop enough wood to make it through the evening and into the night. The kid and his puppy follow me downstairs, chatter and run around but he must know they should be tumbling on a warm carpet in front of a TV or something. My knees ache as we run up and down the hill, lug the logs for the fireplaces.

Then we're inside laughing, spluttering our soup with tales of the day. The three of us plus a not yet housebroken puppy huddle in the nursery. I've got the fire glowing, and I lean into Connie, soft, and welcoming. We close our eyes in front of the dying embers. Eric burrows into his feather bed, his clean room in need of paint, but comfortable. The holiday break provided rest and healing for us all. My bronchitis cleared, as did Connie's pneumonia, but she's still weak.

At dawn Connie gets up and runs downstairs in her fuzzy slippers. Screams in the cold shower. We can't have any gas until she gets a Certificate of Occupancy, and it's not looking good. My hundred cup coffeemaker's boiling water, and a large steel bowl serve as a place to wash chapped faces and hands. Connie's smaller coffeemaker and the hot plate stand by. She grinds her beans, pours water through the filter, spoons out hot oatmeal sprinkled with raisins for the three of us. We're homesteading in the middle of ten million people.

I signed up "for the duration" but actually I have no idea how long a duration is. The boy follows me outside for firewood, his brilliant gold hair fringing out from a blue cap.

"Hey, little buddy, look at this!" It rained last night, and now the contents of the wheelbarrow are frozen solid.

Eric peers into the barrow, reaches out a hand. I don't stop him. "Is it jello?" A puzzled look.

"Nah, it's ice. Come on, we have to break it up." Minutes later we're in the house with cold wood, somewhat dampened in spite of a tarp. When I light the fire, puffs and steam indicate a smoky morning ahead.

Connie's refinanced her construction loans once again, with even heavier interest. No idea how she'll make a June deadline for a Certificate of Occupancy. The woman goes completely quiet when she's panicked, doesn't say a thing. She sped out of the driveway before sunup, going to go buy drywall, then a long commute to her office. I drop the kid at school and head over to the new Catholic Charities center by the railroad tracks. Need some extra muscle today. Haven't spoken Spanish in the three years since I quit restaurant work.

An hour later I pull into the driveway with two guys. Rafael's damp curls form a nest of black hair under the bill of his baseball cap. Clean jeans and T shirt, a spotless navy sweatshirt. Days of plaster dust cover my clothes, a sneeze waiting to happen. An older man follows, sturdy physique, trudges along behind. I pour us three mugs of coffee. *Leche? Sucre?* The three of us head upstairs into the piles of rubbish and broken plaster. Nearly a half-ton of debris sits along the hallways.

"What we're going to do is clean this up and prep it for new sheetrock. We've got to haul all this downstairs into the driveway."

The two laborers look around at the mess upstairs, glance at the double flight of stairs down to the driveway. Rafael speaks, "Mister, I don't see a dumpster."

"No worry. We're going to recycle it."

The older man looks at me, recycle? Shakes his head. *El jefe está loco.*

I pull apart three new plastic trash barrels.

"Let's each grab one of these and clear this out."

Within minutes, Rafael has a full barrel, bounces down the steps, a thirty-gallon load of debris resting on his shoulders. He's tall for a Guatemalan, looks about five-nine, moves like a cat.

I follow in a few moments with my load, heavier and more unwieldy than I anticipated. Damn knees. Catch my balance on the wide staircase. Rafael grabs my can and skips back down the stairs. We step back up, fueled with more coffee, and shovel faster. The second man, short and barrel chested, struggles with his load. Can't lift the trashcan onto his shoulders like Rafael or me. Bends over and picks it up in his arms, hauls it downstairs.

The man takes a break to mop his forehead. Strolls back into the kitchen, heaves a sigh, shuffles toward the stairwell. How old is he? Unlined face, sad eyes, no telling.

"*Hombres! Descanso!* Break Time," I yell up the stairs.

Rafael calls out, "Mister, we don't need a break." In their world, work stops, money stops.

Connie's left us a plate of cookies. "This's heavy work, you must drink water, rest your body." Rafael gets his drink, stands. The older man plops into a chair, stretches his aching back and shoulders. Bends his neck and sighs. No conversation. He's not accustomed to looking a boss in the eye.

We run up and down for another two hours. By late morning, a mountain of debris sits at the side of the driveway.

*"Lonche, vamos a comer!* Let's eat!"

Sometimes laborers get lunch breaks, time to get to a convenience store for a burrito and chips. Often, they work all day.

Our kitchen table offers beef stew left over from Sunday dinner, fresh apples, chips, cookies, and an extra pot of rice. Rafael fills his bowl, packs a second bowl with rice. I offer seconds on stew. Rafi finishes the pot. The kid is seventeen, should be enrolled in high school, could be a track star. Sparkling eyes, unlimited energy—needs to be fed like a good horse.

"This stew, delicious, you make?"

I lapsed into my restaurant Spanish. "I like to cook, started really early. We had seven kids at home."

Rafael's expression grew serious. "My mother and sisters cook like this, but we had twelve. Some days not enough for everyone." Rested his elbows on table, looked into my face. "I come from Guatemala, no work there."

"Did you come here with family?" Don't know why I asked that. Already knew from the kitchens that young men like Rafael get to the U.S. on their own. Many are little brothers who will not be inheriting the farm. He'd just explained that in different words.

"No, I come alone. I live with two other men, like a family." Rafi shook his head. The second man listened to the Spanglish conversation. Also from Guatemala, he's exhausted from heavy manual labor and old injuries. Stories look out from behind his sad face but he won't tell them today.

I break the work at four o'clock. The men look confused, expected work and pay to go until five.

Rafael asks, "Mister, is there anything else we can do? I have time."

"Oh, there's more to do. Follow me."

Clean buckets, rags, and brooms sit in the shop closet. I pick up a broom to sweep the stairwell. "Let me show you how to do clean up. It's part of the job. A good contractor never leaves a mess in someone's home."

We wipe down dust, first with mops, then on hands and knees. Connie's fifty-year old Kirby does the final honors, vacuuming the last bits of dust. She's going to need a shop vacuum, something for wet things, dry things, sticks and nails.

"Guys, quitting time. Let me get you back downhill to Catholic Charities." I pull my wallet out, hand them each fifty dollars.

"Good work. Can you come tomorrow?"

A clean quiet hallway waits for their answer. It could take a month of tomorrows and several men to make Connie's deadline. There's a lot to lose by not trying. The older man looks at all the dirt on his clothes, "*Lo siento*, sorry, I'm busy tomorrow."

Rafael, "Sure! *Mira*, Mister, my house she's at the bottom of this hill. Could you drop me off there instead? I got a couple friends. You can use them? They work hard like me."

I pause, car door open. They won't be vetted by Catholic Charities, but helping hands may be on the way.

"How about I pick you guys up at 8:00 tomorrow?"

Connie gets in from work, picks up Eric at daycare, where he's been playing with friends all afternoon. Opens the fridge, the beef stew has disappeared. Tonight, its canned soup and grilled cheese sandwiches.

"How many guys did you have today?"

"Two, but one of them is a fantastic worker. I don't think he's had a decent meal in weeks. Oh, and he's bringing two more guys tomorrow."

"Come on, let me show you what they did!"

I lead her upstairs. Hazards and rubble, gone, woodwork washed, shiny brown varnish peeking through. Her eyes widen, then her smile, we kiss and I begin to fumble with her. Connie spins around and dashes back down the stairs.

"Good Lord, I need to go shopping!"

She's fled. An hour later she appears with groceries, flips switches on the hot plates. No oven, no prepared foods, too expensive. Stew it is, alternating with a hundred ways to cook beans.

I take Eric up to tuck him in and read a bedtime story. A new volume of Grimm's Fairy Tales, dark green with embossed gold letters, sits on the little shelf of books and toys. Let's make this real. I roar and rumble through the stories of evil dwarves and monstrous queens who sacrifice children. Turns out Eric hates fairytales, situations too close for comfort—stepparents, breadcrumbs, hard work, dust and ashes. Even a black dog. No thank you.

The third night of these stories, he hides the green book.

The nursery fire burns down to embers. Connie and I drift off to sleep. A fire extinguisher pinned into the wall by our bed guards the hearth. Everyone has a down comforter, all's well.

# CHAPTER THIRTY-SEVEN

# THREE AMIGOS
## WINTER 1989

Rafael, Uriel, and Miguel live together in a rooming house. Rafael introduces his two *compadres*. They look at the huge house, fresh paint, raw dirt and rubbish piled up her sides. Kitchen Spanish confirms there's plenty of work, *mucho trabajo*. I pour coffee, hand each of them a new pair of work gloves.

The house mover's ditches still mark our boundaries. The house is set into the bedrock like a bear tooth. A foundation wall extends twelve feet down in front, and Stan's new drainage pipes lie in two neat layers, one three feet down into the ditch, another a foot down. A couple feet of gravel allows the waters to flow through, but the ditches need filling.

We'll fill them with rubble, like medieval builders. Irish waste nothing.

"Amigos, we're going to shovel all that plaster into the wheelbarrow and dump it into the ditch, spread it out a little as we go."

"What about the sticks?"

"That's kindling. I'll use all those in the fireplace. Stack it over by the chimney. That's our woodpile." I'm trying to remember more Spanish. The three guys are Central American, two from Guatemala and one from El Salvador.

Uriel, square jawed and barrel chested, has relentless energy. Two men shovel a load into the barrow. He grabs the handles, moves the load toward the ditch, tips it up, stands in thought. Only a few months before, he stood in a ditch in El Salvador, explosions and gunfire overhead. Friends fell dead in those ditches. *El talishte*, the Tank, goes back for another load.

For three hours Rafael, Miguel and Uriel shovel, dump wheelbarrow loads of broken plaster into the ditch. The lumberyard delivers pallets of drywall to the bottom of the driveway.

I hit the microwave, call for lunch break. A pot of Arroz con Pollo sits on the table, a full chicken leg for each man, vegetables and flavorful rice. The three amigos and I will eat at the kitchen table, too cold to enjoy a view from the new deck. It's not a proper kitchen. There're spots all over old kitchen linoleum. Might be an old pattern, spills of plaster and putty, or some other slurry tracked in? Only the kitchen knows. Kitchen walls? Torn down to lath. Cold, chilly wind blows straight through chinks in old mud and lath. The men sit.

"Your *señora*, she knows meat and potatoes, not *hamburguesa* like Taco Bell."

Of course! She knows food. Not having a stove, now that's a problem. The Gas company won't hook us up until we pass final inspection. That means the new hot-water tank, her 1940 O'Keefe and Merritt range and the clothes dryer sit there, pretend fixtures, like in a dollhouse. Don't even ask about the furnace. No pipes. As it is, we've got a friendly inspector or we'd all be on the street.

The men don't see all this. They look at the table, smile, bow heads. Rapid speech, not sure what they are saying.

"*Gracias, gracias, Señor!*"

"*De nada. Comer!*"

We pass the tray of oranges, cookies, chips, enough for four hungry men.

Miguel's mustache outlines a huge smile, a real job, great food and enough money to save.

"Mister, how old's this house?"

"Oh, about eighty years or so. I'm not quite sure. Connie has all the records."

"But it's your house, no? Why you cut this house?"

Great question.

"Connie moved it here. A bank planned to tear it down. She wanted to save the house."

The three men, who share a single room, look around at broad hallways, the workshop, plus the four big rooms upstairs. Tear it down, when people don't have places to live? Their eyes all meet over the table.

Rafael comments. "Of course we'll save this house. We can help you fix it."

Uriel asks, "So, you do all this for your wife?"

"She's my *novia*, my girlfriend."

Oh, man, I haven't had to explain that, and it didn't come out right. Connie and the little boy are everything to me. Can three people be in love? Then what? Well, you can't be definite about everything in life.

Uriel's eyes widen. Everything he does, all the loads he's lifted this morning, are a promise to his wife and child that he will bring them to Los Angeles one day. He's got many questions of this wandering Irishman.

"Oh, Señor is not the owner?"

How to explain this. I've never owned anything, but these men have grown up on the land, until someone took it away. I grew up on land, but it belonged to my parents. I never thought of staying there to spend my days raking and mucking horse stalls. Uriel looks out over the yard, the empty canyon. I've pulled down the bill of my baseball cap.

"But that's your little boy."

"Uh…um…he's her son."

"No?" Uriel probes further.

"But how can this be? He looks like you, walks like you, works by your side. He listens to everything you say. A son does these things. He's a good boy."

Wait a minute. I've got dark curling hair and a red mustache, nothing like Eric's blond mop. We look alike?

"Why do you do this?"

Good question. I've been hunting down acting roles for almost ten years, gotten some credits, lived the life. Still go out on afternoon auditions. Turned one down—it was going to involve making out with a stranger, and perhaps a little more. Wouldn't do anything Connie couldn't watch and she's been hurt enough.

Connie and I haven't discussed a future. I'm waiting on a call from Martin Scorsese for a starring role in some picture about crime and consequences. She's awfully tired of corporate sales. Am I in on all *this*? Big question.

I change the subject. His question, "Why do you do this?"

"I'm the same as you. Just a different generation of workers."

"*Que paso*? But, you're white!"

"I'm Irish. We came here a long time ago. Actually, my grandad was a cook in a mining camp."

"Like you! And your *novia*?"

"Oh, she's very different. A businesswoman. Wears suits and bosses people around." Stretched my back, stood up. "We're a little bit of everything."

The men do not allow me to pick up dishes, not even a plastic cup. After cleanup Rafael, Uriel and Miguel line up, side-by-side. Rafael speaks, "What now, *jefe*?" We walk the area outside the dining room windows, yard clear of debris, the ditch filled. My little army has done work that I'd scheduled for nearly double these hours.

"Guys, I've got at least a couple month's work for you, if you can come every day from eight to four. Fifty dollars a day in cash, plus meals. We pay on Fridays. That's Connie's banking day."

Smiles all around. The three men pull on their gloves and march out to the driveway where pallets of new building materials wait to go inside.

Two by two they take fifty-pound sheets of drywall upstairs. Two bedrooms, the bath, and kitchen, all need walls. The inspector recommended that we leave the lath and hang the plaster right over it. Less work plus a very sturdy wall.

I love puzzles. We've set up Connie's drafting table in the downstairs hall. The challenge is cutting and fitting pieces into these hallways, passages to everywhere and nowhere. Angles and arches, two turns at stairway landings, and a floor-to-mezzanine ceiling measurement of eighteen feet. No place to set an extension ladder on the stairs.

The rooms? Oversized with angled ceilings under the gables, arches everywhere. Complicated woodwork. At present all the teak is stacked in the shop closet, boards initialed by room, numbered in sequence. It's got to go back in place once the drywall is up.

Miguel and I begin with ceilings. Rafi and Uri, new to plaster work, lift the first heavy sheets overhead, watch each other ascend a couple rungs of the scaffold ladder. The plaster sheet must be set flush against the ceiling. Our mechanical screwdrivers tag screws into each corner, center in on the ceiling joists. Everyone hangs on. Errors here could break even a thick neck.

Within a couple days we've all learned to slap those walls up. Two teams of two men each hang dry wall, spit out nails as fast as Popeye when he's gulped down his spinach.

After a full day's work, school, and day care, Connie, Eric and I assemble in the kitchen again, soup or stew on the hot plate, spoons clanking. Dog napping under the table. Connie changes into a plaster covered sweatshirt. A bucket of joint compound and a blade sit ready for her. Instead of TV, our little family uses hot work lights. Connie tapes seams, spreads the compound, and presses it until the wall smooths out. Other nights she dons ventilator and goggles, sands all the patches and seams until a hand can't feel any ridges. Bits of goop fall off her trowel to dry on the floor. Eric picks them up with a putty knife and builds fanciful worlds of misshapen mountains and cities of old plumbing bits, where his action figures fly and save each other from plastic dinosaurs.

# CHAPTER THIRTY-EIGHT

# SEALING THE UPSTAIRS
## WINTER 1989

I was the girl who had to use every color in the crayon box. When I graduated to paints, I didn't use them like other kids. My senses shimmered with blends of color and light. It wasn't just my eye, colors seemed to communicate through music, through love. So when my mother suggested that we buy five-gallon drums of Navajo White and roll the paint on every surface, I knew she was right. But I don't always do the right thing.

Crunches of time and money—everything needed to be painted new before a Certificate of Occupancy and gas permit could be issued. Mom and my brother were right. I called my brother to thank him for his Christmas gift, a used Wagner Power Painting system, one that he'd used on apartment houses. It's supposed to give a continuous feed of paint so that you don't even need to stop, fill and squeeze your roller. We read all the directions, thinned our paint, fill the tank on the thing. Push the button, a reassuring growl. Squeeze the trigger, wait for paint to come up through the roller. Nope. Sploop, sputter. Nothing. Then a huge squirt splashed out, right across the room.

"Shit!" Chet didn't finish yelling for a good twenty minutes. Damn machine threw paint everywhere—drop cloths, windows, my sweatshirt. Just not on the wall. I grabbed cleaning rags and a bucket. He restarted the machine. Another clog. Took the entire thing apart, checked all the hoses. The motor works. Only thing pumping, adrenalin.

I looked at the mess. It's all I can do to clean this place up. I've got a deadline, or we'll be bank owned.

Not sure why the power roller failed. Head didn't hear its excuses. What did I hear? This old house spoke of a different world, one that resonated with all the colors of nature. I listened to her, of sunsets and sunrises, of trees in the canyon, the twilight of an evening sky. So on a December day I studied my Prussian-blue tiles in the dining room, selected a softer teal blue, one tone lighter than the tile. Imagine my surprise when blue appeared on the bottom level of my scraper, the first identifiable layer of paint. How odd. Someone else envisioned a twilight blue dining room, lit candles bringing the night sky inside.

Saved the white for utility rooms, the shop, the laundry.

The bedrooms stood as empty cubes, not so much as a mattress or pillow in any of them. New plaster dried on the walls, in the crannies. The last residents painted the new master bedroom lavender, now a dingy gray. The bedroom with its porch faces a lush Mt. Washington canyon, hears a dawn chorus of birds. The room spoke of sage green. I picked up the scraper. The first chips flick off my blade, an almost identical match to buckets of sage green paint stacked in the hallway.

I called Andee Rebeck after the third coincidence. Andee wouldn't shy away from ghosts, or whatever guides my instincts. The house wasn't haunted, but as we moved from repair to restoration, she insisted on certain choices, a definite perplex for us.

"Man, what I wouldn't give for a massage right now. This glass of wine will have to do."

Andee asked, "So, what are you guys up to?"

"You're not going to believe this. We've been painting all week. I think I've somehow picked up the original colors of the house."

"Oooh! That's really exciting. How do you know?"

"I'm finding my colors all over old paint chips, almost like messages, you know, stories in old newspapers? That sort of thing?"

"Well, when we're analyzing how to redo a historic property, we peel a few chips. Once you have a chip, pick it apart from the recent color on top, down to the original pigments. I put them under a microscope and look at the layers. Have you looked at them under magnification?"

"Are you kidding me?" I'd had buckets sitting in rooms before we scraped away at the first ancient drips. No, there was no microscope, and no time to play with paint chips.

The guys ran a board the length of the hallway to join up the floor. A maze of crisscrossed lumber and old nails forms the archway, built to last, until the chainsaws came through bisecting the corridor, like a magic trick gone wrong. Somehow the old lady survived the box and the saw.

Feminine elegance shows in the large, graceful arches that swoop across hallways, beckon us into rooms. Even the wall above the fireplace sets back into a gentle curve, an alcove to present an attractive mantle. Chet's confused, very few straight lines in these rooms. How the heck do we drywall the curves?

We have no idea what to do about her big hallway arch. Chet pulls off his facemask and goggles, examines the puzzle. He has straps to connect the wood, but the open frame—how do you begin to do that? Strap the wood, bang up some lath, mud coat and finish coat? Chicken wire? Oh, no. Too much mud comes down.

Miguel steps next to him. Miguel hopes to return to Guatemala to his own farm, chickens, perhaps a mountain place to grow coffee.

"My family house in Guatemala also old, I think many years older than this. Much work. When the rain comes, the plaster breaks, like this." He holds up a handful of broken mud coat mixed with bits of old gypsum and paint chips. "I fix plaster all my life."

Arches and vaults will give him ample chance to prove his skill. The plasterer who can fix this would be able to plaster the moon.

Miguel speaks.

"Mister, I know how to do this."

"How?"

"Like this."

Miguel lifts a piece of scrap drywall, sets it on the plywood worktable. He picks up the T-square, adjusts it on the paper covered plaster, picks up a utility knife. Scores one side, cutting through the paper, but not through the plaster, lifts and bends it. Chet looks on amazed. If you score the plaster every couple inches, it can be bent away from the cuts, but won't break. Miguel calls the other two amigos. They measure the arch, more than eight feet around the bend, and a full four feet deep. Can they score the drywall, lift it, not break it?

Miguel makes the marks. He and Chet lift the piece with the greatest of care, as the other two tack it into the arch. Of course. As soon as the arch is nailed, Miguel mixes the slip coat for his masterpiece.

Eric runs down the driveway, home from school, and he can't wait to sleep in his new room. The paint is dry. Three days ago, Chet covered the bank of windows in newspaper, blue masking tape to protect the edges of the trim.

"Come on little buddy, you can help with this!" They race up the stairs. Chet tugs at the paper and tape, wads it into a ball, throws it toward the trash, misses. Eric rips away at the rest of the newspaper over his windows. Rafael picks up the wads, grabs more paper and tape, wraps on a second and third layer, drop kicks it. It flies. *Futbol!*

Chet grabs the roll of tape, tightens up the ball, sets down two empty paint buckets as goal posts and gives a strong sidekick. He played soccer all through school. Safer than football. Uriel and Miguel join the game, kick the ball toward the paint cans in the L-shaped room. Eric runs behind Chet, squealing as the ball flies through the air. Tries to grab it with his hands.

"No. Like this." Uriel tosses the ball up, hits it with his head. "No hands!"

The ball flies until it lands in a can, game over.

Our amigos leave for the day, all quiet now. A glorious new white arch seals the main hall, where dirty lumber and cobwebs hung open for two years.

We wiped down the drafting table, celebrated the evening with pizza and a bottle of two-buck wine, apple juice for Eric.

# CHAPTER THIRTY-NINE

# GROUNDHOG DAY AND OLD TOMATOES
## FEBRUARY 1989

Eight months ago I stepped through broken rooms, listened to the voices in the walls of this old house. She invited, no, pleaded with me to stay. I joined Connie and we've been cleaning up messes ever since. A genuine pound puppy scampers along behind Eric, a constant companion. Soon, if all goes well, um, actually I have no idea what happens next. That's a tough one. I started out with an entirely different dream.

Upstairs, leading out of the warm nursery where we've been living, the voices are clearer. I pass through an empty hallway and the upstairs bedrooms, places for two or three boys and at least two girls. Light comes through the end of the dark hallway, a large bedroom, its bare lath and missing windows speaking of loneliness. A sleeping porch extends beyond. On January days this space looks out to the mountains beyond with their dusting of snow. This space, our space, romantic and private. We'll do it last.

Connie and I aren't married. In fact, Connie's still legally married, and not to me. My mom and another Catholic friend have already had words with me over that one. I disregarded them. Not going to leave her alone, and she doesn't want me to. Not embracing a commitment either. Connie's dozed off in front of the fire, snoring gently into my shoulder.

My fireplace reverie stops. A sleepy little boy chirps. "Mom, Chet?"

Attention turns to Eric.

"I'm supposed to take a hundred things to school tomorrow."

His mom shakes herself. "Eric, how long have you known this?" She's frustrated, and doesn't want to leave the warmest room in the house.

He wrinkles his forehead. "I forget." No wonder. Other little kids go home to cartoons and snacks. He goes home to change clothes, follow me for chores, chases after workers. I think for a moment, "Little buddy, how about a hundred screws?"

Connie quips, "Have we been counting?"

Mouth works. She's awake now. Then we both laugh.

"Let's go see what we have. Grab your robe, little buddy." Eric's grandma has made him a special robe, wool on the outside, soft velour on the inside. I pull on a sweatshirt and we tromp down the stairs to the freezing cold shop. Tools line up on pegboards and shelves. Jars and cans fill bins. I hand Eric a film can, help him choose a hundred screws, brassy ones, tubby zinc, long and pointed, shiny or rusty. Eric grabs the film can, shakes it, stuffs it into his little red backpack.

I've walked Eric home from school all year. Three o'clock is a great time for me to go for a run, meet him, and chat on the way home. Guy things. Chores we plan to do together. We've built a run for his puppy, a shelter under the new deck, complete with carpets and bedding, protected from the elements. Eric helped me pour concrete into small holes around the back of the house, learned to use a level, held posts straight in order to build a sturdy frame, fence it with heavy wire.

"So, how did your counting go?"

"Fine." Then silence. He's thinking, but I can't ever tell how the bits will connect.

We open the big gate to our dog run, ready for a romp in the canyon. Eric pokes at a gopher hole. Today, February 2, 1989, he learned about the groundhog in school—if it comes out and sees its shadow, then what?

I laughed. "We don't have groundhogs."

"Then how long till spring?" Eric turns to me, a serious expression on his face.

"Chet?"

"Yeah, little buddy?"

"I'm going to give you a hundred days to marry my mom and me." The biggest number he knows pops into the child's head and out of his mouth. He's six. Uh oh. Does Connie know about this?

"OK buddy." I pull back the gate, Eric bounds after the puppy, throws sticks for the dog to retrieve. Cupid's aim, flawless. He's struck me straight through the heart. Neither of us tells Connie about our man-to-man talk.

There is no plan. I've been a bachelor for thirty-five years, got sick and tired of being lonely, also of dating complete nutbars. Not sure where Connie fits in that scenario. She's dragged this house up the hill, and she's the sane one in my life? I work away on the house, takes acting jobs when film projects show up. Connie balances an awkward load of workplace, house, son, lover; one extra husband on the side. Don wanders in and out.

Eric got a shiny new calendar for Christmas, so he ticks off the days. Exactly when did he stop speaking to us? Hard to tell. Little boys can be protective of their mothers, but this little Scorpio goes a step further, an uncomfortable silence in the eye of the storm. Days later he stares into his bowl of dry cereal.

"Mom, could you pass me the milk?"

I hand the milk carton across the table. The kid glares, drops his spoon.

"I'm not talking to you."

Connie looks up at me in shock. Eric slumps in his chair, stares into the bowl.

"Eric, go get in the car." A sullen little boy drags his backpack, shuffles out the door. Connie looks at me, dismayed and a little frightened of her changeling. Why would he defy us?

After Eric's morning outburst, we get to work. A city inspector has given the go ahead for the Gas Company to hook up the stove and clothes dryer, hot water at last! Tonight, a warped Formica counter holds the unplugged hotplate and coffeemaker. A pot goes on the stove, biscuits in the oven. Despite the stained enamel and rust, the sink holds hot water and bubbles. Pitted metal shows through the chrome, but our faucets work. Hot showers come next.

After dinner all three of us share chores. I wash dishes, Connie dries, arranges her blue and white plates in the glass fronted cabinets. Eric clears the table, picks up the broom to sweep.

A sudden streak of blue denim. Eric bolts across the floor, empty handed, fist out. He hits me in the groin, hard as a little guy can. Storms out, a six-year-old in a rage, nothing like a child's tantrum. Slams his bedroom door.

Connie helps me to the kitchen table.

"We need help."

Days warm, Easter's on the way.

Eric can't wait to dive into his basket of treats. Chocolate

bunnies nest in baskets on the table, heirloom embroideries deco-
rate the dining room. He's willing to wear his little ice cream social
suit to church on Easter Sunday, complete with striped jacket and
bow tie. I put on a nice yellow shirt and tie, Connie her favorite
blue silk dress. We've been going to church for months now. I want
a Christian wife, and Connie's agreed to try it out.

The leg of lamb, thawed and covered with rosemary, sits in
the fridge ready to roast in a blazing oven. We head out to church,
flowers, sunshine and singing, but Connie doesn't sing. I'm happy.
Eric chirps away.

We get home, the big door with a flowered wreath stands ready
to welcome us. Connie stumbles in, another stabbing headache. She
curls on the sofa, shoes off, blue dress rumpled and twisted around
her. Nothing prepared her for the morning sermon on Jesus Christ,
the one true Son of God, manifested by his resurrection.

I'm not confused about faith. My understandings of right and
wrong have seen lots of crises. She won't lie to me, but her silence
is worse.

"What's wrong with Mommy?"

Connie can't see a center in all this. Things shake and move,
but they also endure. Why not let our differences hide in plain sight?

"Little buddy, if your mom can believe in love, peace, and
truth, everything will be all right."

She looks up through her tears. We sit down beside her.

# CHAPTER FORTY

# NOT ABOUT TWO

## MAY 1989

For nearly a year Eric and I lived in a Disney romance with Chet. At any point I expected to see Thumper jump out from under the house to let us know how far we'd come. Wildflowers bloomed, poppies, lupine, oxalis and the beginnings of a field of nasturtiums. Rooms of the house glowed with coats of fresh paint. Posts stood up straight again, welcomed each morning.

We had a solid home. Eric's behavior now civil, but what had him so temperamental? The counselor asked me to bring Chet to a meeting.

"So, what can you tell me about your relationship with Connie's little boy?"

Oh dear, here it comes. But not a word about Eric's sulking. Instead, Chet describes the *man talk*.

"Isn't that cute? The way he takes care of his mom? He gave me a hundred days to decide to marry her."

She peered through her glasses at the two of us. "I see. The little boy is looking for a commitment."

We looked at each other. We'd both committed to the house. We'd both committed to Eric, but that's not what he saw. He didn't want Chet to leave us, ever.

"And when was that?" she asked.

"Groundhog day....heh heh."

"...and now it's almost May. So why don't you two get married?"

"Uh..." Chet looks at me.

"Um..." I look at Chet.

"That will be sixty dollars please."

Chet opened his wallet.

Hmmm. Eric had proposed to Chet in earnest. We missed that detail. The kid understood something that we didn't. Where'd he get that idea? Eric beamed, all the hidden chatter of the last two months burbled out at once. He wanted to call his grandmother and announce the news.

I punched the buttons. "*Hi mom?* Yeah, I know it's Thursday, and yes, everything's fine."

Mother asked about a current construction project.

"Well, we saw the counselor today. We're getting married."

Her voice bounced over the wires, thrilled.

"Um, sometime, maybe May 1990? Gives us a year to settle things down. I dunno. Sometime, somewhere, no hurry. Maybe something private, up at Big Sur." For me, any place that would require no work for three days of quiet.

Mom would have none of it.

"The wedding needs to take place in front of your fireplace at Christmas."

"Well, we thought maybe we'd go away, and..."

"A big wedding, with all your friends. My God, look at what you two have accomplished! We have to celebrate in your house."

"But it's not finished. I'm working full time, and I don't see how I can get the house done by fall."

No idea why I whined about that detail. My mother didn't

recognize "can't, don't, won't." Doris understood vision and possibility.

"Honey, it'll never be finished. I'll help you. We'll buy material, sew up drapes, go to the swap meets for furniture. I see wedding things there all the time. I'm coming up on the train Saturday morning. See you 11:00, Union Station."

Doris arrived in time for us to hit our first round of Pasadena estate sales. Elegant manses on Orange Grove Boulevard changed hands, people downsized. Three dollars bought a used pair of sheer curtains, the exact length for the living room windows. An old lady offered up a crate of fifty champagne glasses for ten dollars. A Morris chair in need of new upholstery, a foldout sofa for the upstairs sewing room. *Everything but the kitchen sink*, right? Instead, we found a large pedestal sink for the upstairs bathroom, enamel in terrific shape. That sink went into the pickup truck. Week after week we carted home our treasures.

Our one splurge? An engagement ring for me, a sunbeam for my hands, twists of white and yellow gold. No stones. Imagine a diamond coming off in a mess of plaster or adhesive. Gold resists all types of corrosion, and heaven knows I needed to be corrosion proof. But, my Catholic fiancée said we couldn't get engaged until I got divorced. I phoned Don.

His response? "Congratulations hon! Chet's right about that. I'll pick up the papers."

One more chore: arrange an evening schlep to meet up with Don. Don came up with a novel idea. "Look, how about I meet you at Daniel's shop?" His old high school friend, a jeweler, was making my engagement ring.

Oh dear, I hope this ring works better than the last one.

Gee, that sounded deathly romantic, also practical. The three of us, Chet, Eric, and I, not quite divorced, arrived at the shop. The jeweler started to pull out the little box.

"No, not yet." Don sauntered in the door with the divorce folder.

"Hi Guys…" He ruffled Eric's hair, pulled him to the side counter.

"Hey ya, Daniel." Don greeted his pal, the jeweler.

"Boy, go play over there." Don handed Eric a toy, pointed to the corner of the shop. Set the papers on the counter and pulled out a pen. I signed on all the X's. Eric, occupied with Don's toy, behaved as though all of us had met up for a family outing.

Don and Eric stood to the side while Chet presented my ring.

Don threw his arm around Eric, "Why don't I take the boy out for some pizza, and you guys grab dinner?" He continued, "There's a really nice seafood restaurant on the pier, take your time. Show up at my place around nine?"

Eric couldn't believe it: pizza plus staying up way past his bedtime on a school night. Oh, the privileges of growing up in a post-nuclear family.

Days later Chet came home from substitute teaching at Don's school, one hand covering his pocket.

Dinner sat on lighted burners, my hands full of plates, paper napkins and utensils. I dropped the pile on the table and looked at Chet who continued to fumble with his jacket.

Chet said, "Um, you know how we've talked about the three of us getting married?"

"Sure, the whole thing's Eric's idea," I couldn't keep myself from smiling, "but it's a good one."

"You have a ring now, so I got Eric a kitten." In one hand he held a tiny ball of black and white fluff. We hadn't talked about this, or that I'm allergic to cat dander.

"The kitten's adorable." I smiled, eyes watering as I petted the sweet furry gift. Reached for a tissue, where exactly did I leave my inhaler?

June 10th marked exactly one year since Chet moved in, a perfect time for neighbors and friends to celebrate what we'd accomplished together. Invitations went out announcing the engagement, a request for 1910 period clothing: hats, long skirts, whatever, bring snacks to go with our case of champagne.

Stan and Ina arrived, no mud or debris this time, Ina in elegant linens and George Jensen silver, bearing three damask tablecloths. Lynda and David, she in lavender lace, carried a pair of antique candlesticks. I'd made a calico fit pattern for the 1910 silk ball gown that I planned to get married in. Our dear neighbor Fitz showed up in a University of Michigan 1910 tennis sweater, the real deal, his father's. Our workmen came, Gene in his cap and Frank in a white shirt. Ragtime music started, wine poured.

The vision began in 1985 when I called Dr. Robert Winter, a former professor, and asked him if he could look at my find. Dr. Winter arrived with a Batchelder tile and a copy of his newest book, inscribed, "To Connie and Chet, on their most excellent engagement."

# CHAPTER FORTY-ONE

# THE GARDEN OF MARRIAGE
## JUNE 1989

The road ended at open land, its edge beautifully landscaped in every kind of cactus. All this the work of Erika, an elderly lady who lived in a simple ranch style house. She invited me in, showed me her wonderful collection of paintings and macramé work, large pieces that belonged in galleries.

The real treasure? Her magnificent garden. Picture windows took up the back of her house, revealed a view of the city. Hundreds of cactus orchids hung under trees, spilled over urns, surrounded fountains. She'd spent her life in this garden, but time had come to move to an assisted living apartment.

The prospective owners of the house indicated that they couldn't care for her treasures. Well, we had a large bare property, didn't we? Would Chet and Connie help her pack in exchange for her plants? You bet we would! And so began our journey into the world of epiphytes.

We transferred several truckloads full of plants from her garden, shared them with our neighbors. Erika brought us back to help with her garage, more gifts. An enormous macramé would hang from the ceiling of the two-story mezzanine hallway.

I'd assumed that decorating Owl's Nest would be at least a decade down the road. The house filled up fast with treasures precious to Chet and me. We now had six months to prepare for our wedding.

It was time to accomplish formal introductions to Chet's family and friends, an endless drive up to Chico at the north end of the Central Valley. San Joaquin Valley heat feels like the edge of Hades. You can't see the flames, but you breathe them in and out all day long. No moist evenings, no shadows until very late at night. When we arrived, we did not pull up to his mother's big house across from the park. Instead, we showed up at a tidy modern home, not at all what Chet described.

Chet gave me a quick kiss. "I'm going to go do some things at Mom's. You stay here and I'll be back for you." Why the mystery? I didn't know a soul in Chico, but apparently Chet had a plan. His dad held open a screen door, invited me inside. I towed in my weekend bag, no idea where I or the bag might belong.

It had been a long, hot drive. "Would you like a glass of wine?" Chet's dad pulled a chilled white out of the fridge, poured two glasses, handed one to me. Every movement, every word, from Clifford Hood, M.D. had precision and careful thought behind it. The wine, cool and crisp, did its job, but the intense blue eyes searched my face, analyzing.

"So, what happened to your first marriage?"

Bam, direct. Let's get on with this interview. I guess the doctor wanted to know what hurt, but I hadn't come prepared to talk about Don.

I held my breath for a moment, exhaled, realized I'd not prepared myself to discuss the sad parts. What did I walk into? Thought we'd come here to celebrate. Took a gulp from my glass.

"Um, my ex, Don had, still has, a drinking problem. He's a good guy at heart, but I couldn't spend my life—he'd keep going back and forth with the bottles, so I went to Al Anon, and realized Don would never change, might never get better."

Chet's dad locked eyes with me, said. "Chet's mom's an alcoholic. And you're right, I couldn't spend my life that way either."

My fantasy of his family, Chet grew up with it all. The big house, two parents, seven kids, shopping trips to San Francisco for clothes and toys. Chet never misled me, but I didn't understand what "keeping the house" had cost his mother. Their home had nine bedrooms. Three were occupied, and the rest was storage for people who had moved on to their own lives. His two youngest brothers both lived at home, worked night shifts. Our midafternoon arrival coincided with breakfast time for them. Chet picked me up for the formal introduction.

For more than a year Chet described a home of rose gardens and fruit trees. The courtyard held a few surviving trees in pots, several plants dried out in the heat. The Spanish garden long gone. Oranges on their trees froze, roses died. An airplane propeller stood in a corner. My future mother-in-law sat at a picnic table in her courtyard, cooling down from the heat of the day. Next to her chair, the stepladder she used in place of a walker. She'd been ill for years. I didn't really understand her situation, because I'd never been around the ravages of rheumatoid arthritis. I'd walked past wheelchairs for years, not thinking about the people inside crippled bodies.

The two youngest brothers took care of her, but they had not grown up in the same household as Chet. They'd both stayed home, worked blue collar jobs right out of high school, saved the house and their mom.

When the shadows darkened the area, Chet lit a hibachi to celebrate July 4th with hot dogs and beer. Shorts, tank tops, slapped at some bugs. Peace, truth, love made up the core of this family, in sickness and in health. I now knew what Chet wanted, and why he was willing to work so hard for our dream house on the hillside.

# CHAPTER FORTY-TWO

# WEDDING

## DECEMBER 1989

*Wedding is great Juno's crown,*
*O blessed bond of board and bed.*
*'Tis Hymen peoples every town,*
*High wedlock thus be honored.*
*(Wm. Shakespeare, As You Like It)*

The house shimmers. Quarter-sawn oak floors glow under afternoon light. Refinished them about two weeks ago. A new copper screen shines in front of the fireplace. A gift from mom, who hoped that the light would never go out of this union.

A Christmas tree in the corner, its hundred wax candles sitting straight in their holders, ready to be lit. Eighteen months of work have led to this night. Chet installed strands of white icicle lights along the eaves. A massive fresh wreath hangs on the broad oak entry door.

The wreath, an unexpected gift. When we went down to the train yards to find the enormous tree, one with strong straight limbs, a tall worker asked why I was so particular about the branches. I explained an inherited family custom, live candles.

"Are you German?"

"Not really, but I speak it."

"Do you know 'O Tannenbaum' in German?"

"Sure"

His dark face glowed in the string of bare lightbulbs. "Would you teach it to me? We have a party the night of Christmas Eve, when these sell out."

For the next several minutes the two of us sang in the tree lot until he knew the German words. He walked me up to the front and lifted out a huge fresh wreath for the new front door of our home. A wedding present.

Garlands of greens and yards and yards of heavy white embroidered ribbon swag to announce *our new family*. Grandma Hood's gift? Old fashioned strands of pearl and crystal beads, white ornaments.

There's magic in marriage. I studied 1910 ball gowns in old photos, bought sixteen yards of off-white raw silk. For eight months a sack of embroidery projects accompanied me everywhere, original designs of Celtic knots for my Irish love, a bond that would never untie. During long nights I planned, cut, fitted a cotton mock-up, then cut into the precious raw silk. Tante Sofia sent Amsterdam lace for a veil, an eighty-year-old bolt left from my grandmother's stash.

Upstairs, women gather in the pink room, a carpeted, soft, secret place. I sewed my gown and Chet's jacket in that room, worked long nights to shed any lingering doubts. This afternoon, one more touch of the curling iron, tuck every curl under a veil. My French aunt cries out, "Parfum! She needs Parfum!" Our matron of honor, Andee, disappeared a few minutes ago. She's busy short sheeting the bridal bed. Ha!

Doris greets guests in the burnished hallway, her silver and garnet brocade suit dripping with strings of real jewels. Through the big door come women in long gowns, men wearing tuxedos, more jewels. One aunt in amethysts and another in sapphires. I'm wearing grandmother Westervelt's crystals with my wedding gown.

Everything sparkles. Even the sounds.

Faye's golden harp picks up the light of the fire. Next to her Lynda and David are tuning a violin and cello. Chet hears the commotion but doesn't listen. His quest is fulfilled, ready to proclaim in front of God, family and friends.

He stands by the fireplace, roaring gold flames, a darkened room. Little Eric stands beside him beaming—a new daddy, a puppy and a kitten. The two of them hold long taper candles, a third ready for mom when she comes downstairs. The first strains of music pick up.

His day hasn't been perfect. Furnace guys balked at having to complete the hookup on a Saturday. Had to force the issue. He hasn't seen the gown but knowing Connie it would involve a décolleté neckline and bare shoulders. Furnace is now hooked up—blazing hot in the living room, no heat anywhere else. He'll deal with the ductwork later. Our maxim?

"If you're in the kitchen and you get cold, you're not working."

"If you get cold in the dining room, you're not drinking."

"If you're cold in bed it's your own damn fault."


At last he'd had a quiet hour to catch his breath before the minister arrived, reflect on what changed in eighteen months. The grand and cozy master bedroom offered an open view of the canyon, green trees and the snow-capped Angeles Crest. A perfect winter afternoon sunset. The best man popped a champagne cork over the railing and it flew.

A knock at the bedroom door. Connie's brother Ron, chef's apron tied over his dress slacks and white shirt, a worried look on his face. Ron and his wife organized the buffet for a hundred guests, just as we did for their wedding a few months ago.

"Chet, there's no water. A workman from your neighbor's came by, said something about breaking a pipe."

Our new copper pipe! Some clods of workmen struck it with the pickaxes. This would have never happened if they'd used shovels and a little care.

Chet shot out of the chair and ran down the stairs, Ron on his heels heading for the street and a geyser of muddy water. The neighbor's workers stood aside.

"Hey, sorry mister, we're just going to have to shut off the water, almost five o'clock. Somebody come fix everything Monday."

Chet, dressed in his Edwardian jacket and boutonniere, jaw set, a growl and a glare. Connie's brother, six-foot-seven with a chest like a brick wall, towers over the group.

"I'm getting married at five o'clock, about forty-five minutes from now. You have half an hour to fix this."

"OK mister, we could clamp and patch it for now?" The guy's sweat formed under the bill of his cap ran down his face. My two men turned back to the house.

Catering duty called. Ron headed back into the kitchen, carried platters of food and a hundred glass plates to the buffet tables. White roses, mint leaves, and cranberries decorated the wedding cake, already installed alone on a table at the dining room windows, framed by Laura Ashley lace curtains. Sealed the pocket doors to keep kids and dogs away from the feast.

At last, moments of perfection. Errors put aside. Fireplace roaring, and the pastor delivering a ceremony that we'd all written together. From the darkened room, a fireplace and our three tapers glowed, until we lit all the candles and the Christmas tree. In lieu of a prayer, we asked our friend David to play a Bach Suite for cello, a chance for us to meditate and breathe during the ceremony. For fifteen minutes Chet gazed at me, every inch, fully gowned and veiled and also bared to my soul.

Half an hour later, I reached for the pocket doors to welcome a hundred guests to our feast. Stopped, stared at my golden wedding ring. Smiled, and brushed away the tears.

# CHAPTER FORTY-THREE

# CANOES AND KITCHEN SINKS
## SUMMER 1990

Connie and I were both born on Great Lakes, grew up on the waters. The canoe's our favorite ride. After you push off the waters deepen, forceful eddies and currents keep the boat on the move. I taught my wife how to steer from the back seat, paddle directly into waves. We took turns propelling from the front. Lead and follow, the ultimate test for marriage.

Within two years Connie and I'd become full partners. Whether we're on the water, or huffing lumber up a dry hillside, we've learned to take turns leading and following each other, accept errors and wrong directions as part of our adventure.

My dad offered us a DIY kitchen remodel as a wedding gift. Our hodgepodge of a kitchen, was a hot mess, but we'd eaten there for two years.

The kitchen is the engine of a home and it's by far the hardest room to take apart and rebuild. Water, gas, and electrical do jobs that used to take hundreds of hours of gathering fuel and pumping. We wanted to keep period features, but everything needed to function.

Owl's Nest's bones were perfection; roomy cabinets, tin-lined storage bins, rock maple counters that stretched on forever. Surprises lay one underneath the other. We tore up the linoleum to reveal a Douglas Fir plank floor, like the ones in museums. A ceramic tiled stove base sat intact from 1909.

Connie spent days reading house porn, slick heavy magazine pages of utilitarian kitchens in old houses. She dreamed of a dishwasher, clean tiled counters, a tiled wall behind her 1940 stove, a nod to change over time. We'd save money by doing the demo and clean up ourselves. I knew how to unclog a toilet; Connie had never done plumbing. This job would involve pulling the kitchen sink.

No stilettos today. My wife came downstairs in jeans, paint splattered shirt, and old running shoes. "So, where do we begin?" Hadn't bothered to brush her unruly hair, which often looks like the back end of a Golden Retriever.

"Water shut-off. We need to get under there, in the cabinet. Otherwise we'll have Old Faithful in here."

"So, we shut it off at the sink, not outside?"

"Yep!" I looked at the cabinet, and what needed to happen. "Connie, can you get down there? Feel for two football shaped valves. One's hot, the other cold. Turn off both of 'em."

She succeeded, grabbed her wrench, disconnected the joints, tossed the pieces out of the cabinet.

"Leave that snaky accordion hose—we'll reuse it."

We pried off the 1950s remodel of Formica kitchen counters, unscrewed the hinges from plywood cabinets. More scrap lumber, but who knows what's in that paint? Thick hardwood remained under all the cabinetry, throughout the pantry. Hardware covered with gunk. I set up the kitchen table for Eric, a drop cloth and several layers of newspaper. His job?

"Buddy, your mom's gonna toss pieces in that crate."

"Um huh?" Big eyes under the baseball cap, looked at the crate.

"You're gonna take them apart and clean them." Eric ran back and forth, grabbed the hardware, sat down with his little wrenches and a can of WD-40. The battered shop radio piped out the jazz station this morning, great beat. Eric pulled out his wire brushes and steel wool, scrubbed away in time to the music. Scraped off the grime and rust, cleaned the bits. Put them back together to see if they worked, dropped the repaired pieces into Connie's old baking pans.

Pulling the sink came next. My wife and I both had strong backs. We braced ourselves on opposite sides of the thick corroded pipes, set the wrenches and pulled in opposite directions. Nothing. One defiant hunk of rusted metal.

"This's fuckin' stuck!" Treated the galvanized mess with WD-40, pulled again. Hit the wrench with a hammer, it groaned, but corrosion sealed those pipes. Connie's so right. We've gotta replace all this with PVC and copper.

A theatre trust exercise seeped up through our memories. With the counter gone, the two of us could stand, set our pipe wrenches around the damn thing, my wife ready to swing left, me to twist to the right. Steel reinforced boots set toe to toe. Eyes locked, and using ourselves as a pair of hefty counterweights, both leaned back at the same time, gripping the wrenches. A stumble or slip would definitely mean an ER trip. The pipe groaned, then the threads slowly turned, until Connie could steady the sink while I unscrewed it.

We'd now destroyed our clean and functional kitchen.

We scrubbed and repainted inside the cabinets, walked back and forth in a fresh space. On Monday, the clanking of tools and shoving of large cardboard boxes announced our plumber delivering a dishwasher, a sink and a garbage disposal. No countertop yet. Eric climbed into the cabinet, examined all the new pipes.

There's a sensuality in watching a woman handle power tools, the way she sways, runs her hands over the finished surfaces. In the evening Connie masked up, got out the heat gun to attack the pantry. Her heat gun and paint scraper melted the old paint. Okay, she also liked methylchloride, but every girl needs her vices. A few rolls with the belt sander and clear wood cabinetry came through, like the kitchens in the Pasadena houses.

What else can we expect from a little girl who used to put Elmer's glue on her arms as zombie makeup, just so she could peel it off? Let her pick away. Sanded and varnished, the cabinets would stand ready to see another hundred years of family use. Evenings well spent.

I cut a new plywood counter for her tilework, repaired drawers. Ceramic squares, tile cutter, hundreds of little plastic spacers sat in boxes on the floor. Watched her mark center lines, work outward until a couple inches from the edge. Then, the snap of her tile cutter. Fit the corners.

I went for a Saturday morning run. Detoured at an estate sale, all sorts of items laid across an old oaken table.

"Is that table for sale?"

"I didn't think about the table. My parents bought it second hand in 1928."

Bingo. Antique. My wife will go nuts over this thing. What's in our checking account? 'Guess how many marbles in this jar?' I tried a number.

"Will you take $300? I'm restoring the big brown house across the hill over there." Pointed to Owl's Nest.

"Oh goodness, the one they moved?" Her eyes twinkled under her glasses.

I nodded, smiled at her.

"You know, there's four chairs hanging in the garage? Would you like those too?"

"Let me go get a truck. I'll be back with that and the money in about an hour."

Ran home, drained our account. Got back there with the truck.

"Oh, thank goodness! Everyone's been asking about the set since we brought down the chairs. A dealer came by and offered me $900."

Shit. I should have cashed her out right when I saw it, but I don't carry a checkbook in my running shorts.

"... but I told her I gave it to the young couple fixing up the old house over there."

I couldn't keep a big grin off my face. Ah, the Luck of the Irish.

# CHAPTER FORTY-FOUR

# FILLING THE NEST
## FALL 1990

Puff, puff, puff....

My daily run, a two-mile loop. Stopped at the elementary school, leaned over, hands on knees, caught my breath, wiped off the sweat with my bandanna. Eric shouted, ran to the playground fence. We walked home every afternoon, a time to catch up on "man talk." My third grader had a forty-year-old mind in a seven-year-old body.

"Chet, when are you and mom going to have a baby?" He'd prepared his questions. His friends had little brothers and sisters. He wanted one. He even knew how to give bottles and change diapers. Learned at day care.

"Oh, little buddy, I don't know...whenever babies come."

Eric stared at the ground intent on cracks in the sidewalk, a few acorns here and there. My answer to him, unsatisfactory. A dog and cat not enough for this little guy?

"Look. I've been an only child for seven years, and that's too long." He hit the nail on the head. Time to fill the nest.

I put my arm across his thin little shoulders. Why not? Connie sure drops a great baby. I dreamed of a little girl for us, energetic like the Hoods, clever like her mom. I even named her, my initials, Colleen Joy. Then another one, a little boy if there was time. She turned forty last summer. Time to fill our house.

Connie's plan sat on a different vector. She thought we should rent out rooms, the nursery and perhaps the pink room, defray expenses. Redo the bath between those two rooms. Fine. Babies take nine months anyway. We'd get right at this, probably have a baby by summer.

Six months later, still no baby in sight and a series of unfortunate doctor's visits. My wife lay on a table, terrified, in great pain, squeezed my hand.

"Do you want to dump me and turn me in for two twenty-year olds?" She blinked back tears.

Godalmighty, a wife's not a used Volkswagen in a wrecking yard. Disappointed? Yep. Pissed off? You bet. Life's not fucking fair. I squeezed back, turned my head away.

Connie and Eric made me happy, even if we didn't have as many kids as some of his friends. Breathe. Count my blessings. Swallow the bitter along with the sweet.

That summer Connie recuperated on the upstairs deck overlooking the open field. Time for a back yard, not a public hiking trail across our land. Took out the axe and started splitting rails, hot sweaty work, then humped my way back up the hill, made lunch and a drink. Eric ran up the rest of the way with her tray. Connie read a novel a day, looked over the porch railing, waved, went back to her books.

Glad I knew how to build a fence. Man, did that bring back hot summer days in Chico. Raging, blistering heat. Pounding away at dry dusty soil with a posthole digger. Damn thing's a ten-pound steel bar, shaped like a toothpick. By the fifth time you slam it into hard ground, it's a fifty-pound weight. Maybe get one hole to pour in cement, set a fence post. Do it again.

In my entire life, I had one fight with my dad, me about fifteen. Suffocating heat, over a hundred degrees. Dad and me repairing a break in the fence. Horses got out. So much for time with my friends.

When I hit that rock, it rang throughout my entire skeleton. White pain seared from my feet to my teeth.

Threw the posthole digger and yelled, "Fuck this place!"

Dad didn't ignore my cry. He worked the ground a couple posts away, maybe twenty feet. In slow motion, two huge leaps, caught me mid-stride on the third. Grabbed me by the belt and the scruff of my neck—lifted me above his head and then slammed me down into the ground. Knocked all the air out of my lungs.

Leaned down into me, face to face. "This is your land, this is your home. Don't you ever talk like that again." Dad turned and went back to work.

The new split rail fence around Owl's Nest would take some fifty post holes. Spent a month pounding that fucking earth while the princess was upstairs reading her books asking for little salad lunches.

White rage can clean you out. Connie and I knew fate. Life isn't fair. How do you tell a seven-year-old who's seen his share of disappointment? Eric's serious little face, no tears, processed everything. Taking it like a little man.

Those fence posts became my wrestling match with God. As a kid, I shouted at the heavens. Now my first conflict with the almighty turned out a fucking draw.

When Connie recovered, I couldn't stop her. She wanted a flagstone path. She bought the stones and hauled them down the railroad tie steps herself. Afraid she'd bust her incision. That woman's one tough princess.

Dad drove down again to see how we were doing. While

I cooked, he and Connie stood on the back deck, iced tea with fresh mint leaves from the garden. Dad looked at the fence, then at Connie.

"Did Chet build that?"

"Yes, isn't it wonderful? He says it's like the ones you guys had in Chico."

"Did he use a posthole digger?"

She studied Dad, knew he never asked a question without a reason.

"Yes." She thought everyone built their fences with one of those steel monsters.

"I see."

Connie held her breath. She knew of the 1969 fight. Dad looked out over our land, no expression. Serious.

I didn't turn my wife in for the two twenty-year-olds.

# CHAPTER FORTY-FIVE

# THIS IS LOS ANGELES
## SUMMER 1992

O ne of the treasures of Los Angeles is its people. It made sense to share our home. Young roomers—artists, teachers, graduate students, filled out our merry band, gave me a few opportunities to offer a bit of mothering.

Our only requirements: a passable credit rating, no smoking, and no drugs. Eric monitored everything else, including how many boyfriends a girl could have at a time. The dog selected prospective roomers. A wag and licks indicated, "This person's OK." Tail between the legs? A definite veto. I've misjudged characters many times in my life. Never seen a dog do that.

Often parents did the final sign off and wrote the check. A darling girl came by, said "yes," passed the sniff test. Her Korean parents came to visit, very formal, looked successful. I figured we're home free. Chet lived at a military outpost in Korea in the '70s, could even greet them in GI Korean. *An yeo hasib nikka!* "Hello there!" Worked for picking up girls in military bars. Apparently not right way to say "Good Afternoon" in polite company. Supposed to be *An ya haseo.* Sounded very nice to me.

Jeannie came down the stairs, upset, close to tears.

"What's wrong?"

"You're not going to believe this. Stupid. My mother's *so* superstitious, she believes in the old ways."

Rubbed my forehead, looked at the young woman. Jeannie didn't look back up at us.

"Jeannie, what is it?"

"Mother says the house sits wrong, it's turning, things face the wrong way. I'm so sorry."

I'm standing there mulling, what's our visitor feeling? Yes, Owl's Nest sometimes has a mouthful of things to tell people, but her ghosts are very, very nice, protective and helpful.

The house spoke, reminded me of something. "Jeannie, your mother's right. I moved this house here four years ago. It used to be down in the canyon, in front of that red barn. This house faced the other street. Someone moved it before that, oddly enough from a street near Koreatown. I think it's set right now, but it's been through a lot. Chet and I, we're restoring the home."

She looked from one of us to the other, wide brown eyes, obviously upset and tired of hunting for a place to live.

"I'll go tell her." Slow steps in the stairwell.

I knew very little about Feng Shui, but here's what I understood. We're all living on a magnet, flying around the universe with other magnets. Why wouldn't our physical orientation matter? Who knows how this connects to ancient understandings. Maybe Jeannie's mother has senses the rest of us never heard of. Interesting.

Three sets of footsteps started down the stairs, a clunk on the broken tread near the bottom. Didn't know what went through their heads about us. Another crazy mother, just what Jeannie needed.

"We'll take it."

We lived our dream, working on our home, improving our surroundings by the week. Lovely items appeared at Pasadena estate sales, second-hand drapes in raw silk for three dollars and Oriental rugs offered comfort and beauty in every room. Owls Nest filled up, with people, languages, humor and shared worries.

Only one serious obstacle remained, my death struggle with City Hall. Losing was not an option. If the title wasn't cleared, we'd could end up forfeiting our home. The bank couldn't close our mortgage paperwork and the construction lender would take all. Problems started with rocks in the road that soon became boulders, the specter of Grading Division. They approve hillside developments and streets in new tracts. Grading wouldn't sign their own inspection because they adhered to an obsolete parcel map, a tract with winding greenbelts and cul-de-sac streets. Civil servants became greedy serpents, slithering out from between the paths, blocking anyone who wanted to get anything done. They lied, they swindled, and they ate $100 bills before they opened reports.

Each subsequent owner of the canyon kept the ten-year-old development application active, lovely drawings of an imaginary community on the old ranch land.

A city functionary claimed that our address was "a high-class alley" and that it needed lights and sidewalks. The cost of rebuilding the "high-class alley" would be far in excess of what I'd paid for our house. Grading permits had already cost an astounding $41,000 before we even touched dirt.

I decided to contact Downey Savings, the original owner and see if they knew a real estate lawyer.

They'd sold the land, which now belonged to a Chinese law firm. Maybe those lawyers would be willing to help us? A new development plan was in process, and they certainly didn't want the home I'd purchased years before. They were in process of submitting new maps and included our separate parcel map in all their submissions to the city. Another year passed, but they didn't break ground.

It was on a spring afternoon that Chet and I were sitting upstairs, reading and enjoying a pot of tea.

What's that?

We looked down into the fields, long grass growing, a bit of mustard and oxalis peeping through. Flashes of gold and yellow, then a procession coming up the road, past the caretaker's cottage, around the stables, into a field of wildflowers where we'd often held Easter Egg hunts. The men were bald, shaved heads, long saffron colored robes, lanterns full of incense. They stepped over the foundations where the house had lain, looked up the hill. Behind them followed some dark-haired men in business suits.

What on earth are we looking at? I have no idea what was said in their ceremony, but a week or so later the local paper announced that the canyon had been sold to the Santa Monica Mountains Conservancy and was to become an Urban Wilderness Preserve.

The Feng Shui had led them in the right direction. I dearly hoped that someone would hear us soon.

# CHAPTER FORTY-SIX

# RAFTERS
## WINTER 1992

My boyhood kingdom was Grandma Hood's attic, a place where the younger kids could not go. The attic's mystery and adventure waited for me alone. Inside the door I could stand straight, shine my flashlight on racks of clothes, hatboxes. Bent over, I crawled through Christmas decorations until the beam lit up odd shapes, wooden tennis rackets, ice-skates, and, in its case, a violin. Allowed to bring down one thing, I'd choose a treasure and grandma would tell the story. I chose the violin. Never forgot that moment. The violin belonged to my dad when he played it in elementary school.

This year, when Eric asked for a violin, I knew whom to call. Grandma shipped it to us. Eric spent hours with that fragile piece of wood and wire, trying to make sounds on it. Within a couple months I could whistle the entire first Suzuki book by memory.

For years dirt held Owl's Nest together, layers of hardened dust, wasp nests adhered to eaves. For five-hundred days the dear old house complained, "I'm worn out, the stairs feel crooked to me, the doors stick."

But now, no more complaints. On this night Owl's Nest shared our contentment. I looked around our living room, warm and inviting in spite of torrential winter rains. Sat reading by the fireplace while Connie and Eric practiced.

Suddenly, we heard a crash above our heads. "What happened?" The three of us ran upstairs. Racing through the house, we opened doors, looked around rooms, slammed them shut again. Connie opened the pink room, looked fine, glanced over to the right, not fine. Water drained through the ceiling plaster right onto the new carpet. Pieces of our new drywall lay in wet crumbles on the rug.

"Shit!"

I joined Connie at the doorway.

"No one come in here! Eric, run and get the hard hats, the ones by the cellar door!"

Bounding up the three steps to the bathroom and the trapdoor into the attic, I pulled a chair to stand on—no time to go get a ladder. Climbed through. Found a board to set across the ceiling joists. Stepped along the plank, hoped it wouldn't tip up and smack me in the face like a kid's teeter totter. On either side half-inch wet drywall, now soft, lay between the ceiling joists. I had to watch where I stepped or go splat on the bedroom floor.

"Ow!" Hit my head on something very hard.

From downstairs, I heard, "Chet, are you okay?"

"Yeah, head's hard."

Connie called back, "We're going to need tarps! Eric, thanks for the hats; stay out of the room!" Heard her thumping down the stairs, through the kitchen and the cellar door. Felt my head. Dry. This's gonna leave a bump. My flashlight beam struck rough bark. Never saw lumber like this *inside* a house. Three full-size tree trunks ran the length of the attic, bark still on. Ran my hand along the heavy beams, huge Douglas firs. Biggest one runs the entire sixty feet of the house. Man, talk about *built like a brick shit house*. Nobody has lumber like that anymore.

Listened for the water close by. Couldn't see anything up through the roof, but we definitely had leaks. Three or four, but not on the joint where we'd strapped the house together and re-shingled the roof. Water drizzled a couple feet away, parallel to the seam. The peak of the roof was definitely compromised. What the hell? Did other shingles come loose, and we didn't see them? Inspectors didn't see this either. The rain didn't stop.

Connie yelled, back from the cellar, stepped on the ladder, passed up one tarp through the opening so I could spread it out and stop water coming through the ceiling. She and Eric began to pick up the fallen plaster. The boy's got his hardhat on. Good thinking. I rubbed my forehead again.

"Honey, hurry down to the kitchen and open the cabinets. We need Chet's giant trays, the big kettles." Eric dashed downstairs, roused kitchen clatter enough to bring the hounds of hell.

Thunk, klunk, thunk, thunk.... She's hauling the Shop Vac up the stairs. That thing will do any job wet, dry, or otherwise. Quiet, then the scream of the vacuum, debris hurling into its canister. Connie yelled above it.

"Eric, just bring one at a time!" Right. He's got two or three of my kettles stacked in his arms. This kid thinks a steel mixing bowl makes a dandy hat. Only problem is, he can't see the steps.

The first pots arrived. Connie set one or two under the dripping areas. How many days before mildew sets in? We're going to need some kind of dehumidifier in here.

The following morning we woke to sunshine and inspected the damage. Even with two layers of shingles adhered in place, the roof leaked like a sieve, drained storm water and debris right through the attic.

Connie's determined to hire a roofer. The woman's not a climber. Gets dizzy if she stands on a chair. She's made it very clear that I'm not to go up there either, obviously something is unstable. She's probably not wrong, but that doesn't solve the problem. Her brother's VW bug pulled into our driveway. Giant Ron followed me into the attic, no ladder needed, he felt the ceiling and inspected the leaks. He knew his sister's temper and he knew she damn well couldn't afford a new roof this week.

"I've got an idea. We'll get on this while Connie's going out to City Hell. She'll be gone for hours. Bet we could tarp up the roof before then."

"I'm game. She's right though, how do we stay safe?"

Eric's eyes turned into saucers. I pulled a hank of rope out of a work tub.

"I got us a new rope, seventy-five feet. We're going to tie one end of the rope around my waist, the other around yours. I'll go up first and climb over the gable."

Eric piped up. "Mom said she's hiring a roofer. She doesn't want you to go up there."

Ron studied me, quiet. My eighty-nine-year-old grandfather was still cleaning roof gutters on his house, Ron followed his grandfather onto three-story roofs more than once. "So, Chet, what's our plan?"

"I'm going up and over the peak. You stay on this side, bring the roll of plastic up to the roofline. Once you get your footing, you throw me the roll of plastic sheeting. I'll start covering the area, if you can grab some of these wood strips to batten it all down." Ron and I put on our toolbelts, hard hats, and knotted the rope around our waists.

Eric shook his head. Our designated thinker knew what Mom said. Pretty sure she had a different idea. But mom wasn't home.

"Chet?"

"What?"

"What if Uncle Ron falls? You said it's slippery up there."

"Oh, if he falls, I'll jump."

All Eric could see in his mind's eye? Two grown men hanging off the roof, each with a rope around his waist.

"But what should I do?"

"You're our phone guy. If we fall, you call 911."

Eric stood on the deck, phone clenched in his fist. Listened and watched boots on the extension ladders, didn't move a muscle for the next two hours.

# CHAPTER FORTY-SEVEN

# NOT ABOUT TWO
## FALL 1992

Don called himself the *extra husband*. The two of us joked about our post-nuclear family, one that didn't blow up anymore. Don saw me as a brother, something he'd never had. Wrong. You're not supposed to fuck your sister.

I once suggested that the Connie and Don write a divorce manual. Here's what I learned from their divorce. Connie would eat shit and die before she'd let any harm come to Eric. So would Don. None of this crap with playing parents against each other. Eric knew this too. Any time he tried to manipulate one of us, we called a Family Conference at the kitchen table to come up with a common decision. He hated those.

Sunday afternoon drop off, a big deal. Don's new wife made Eric change clothes when he went to Don's because she said his clothes looked shabby. Eric put on his Nordstrom togs and went to restaurants, Don changed him back into his jeans and T-shirt to come home. Eric jumped out of Don's Jeep, dashed through weeds, down the railroad tie steps toward the dog run.

Don watched Eric chase his dog down the trail to our home-made tree fort. Eric and I had a blast building that fort out of scraps, teaching him how to hammer. Don turned directly toward me, looked me in the eye, "You're sure great with kids."

Where was this going?

"Look you two, if Chet's going to raise my son, he needs to get a real job."

Connie's smiled disappeared. Uh oh. Her one gripe, Don always had something to complain about, something to correct, somebody to blame.

"Chet, the district's short on teachers. You've got a Masters, right?"

"Well, yeah, the degree's in theatre, I still go on auditions."

For ten years I'd lived and breathed auditions. I always got by, worked odd jobs, acting, cooking, and a half-time job in adult day care. I joked to friends about waking up one day to find myself with a wife, a dog, a boy, and a big broken house. Don never said anything straight up. What was his plan?

"You'll need to have your signature on Connie's mortgage. I want my name off title. They'll want your name on. You're her husband now."

I was puzzled. It was her house.

The light dawned. Connie and Don owed Chuck $71,000, without interest. When did I become part of that debt?

Don stood in the kitchen, arms crossed, ankles crossed, leaned on the newly refinished kitchen shelf. Varnished wood cabinets above held shining blue and white dishes.

"So, can you make sure that your auditions take place after 3:30?"

This sounded better and better, a maybe pretty good idea. I'd never given much thought about life after acting. Actors joke about graying hair and cookie guts. Not male ingenue material any more, and Connie wouldn't like that much anyway. Gray hair, yes. Cookie gut—well, I like cookies. Also, popcorn, and maybe beer.

"I can check with my agent, sure."

"If we get you on the sub roll, you can take a day off whenever you're shooting."

"What do I need to do?"

Don unfolded his arms, grabbed a bentwood chair, straddled the seat.

"Get down to 450 N. Grand tomorrow and begin the application process. I'm going to write your letter of recommendation. It'll take them six weeks for your fingerprints and FBI clearance anyway."

The bank application process stalled. A Vice President, interested in old houses, would help Connie with the non-compliant title and the mess with the city. One mess led to another. The banker looks at the super-secret credit file. "Your wife likes to shop." Connie's head snapped around, did I hear the crack?

Excuse me? The credit report showed all sorts of retail accounts, stores we never heard of. What? Also, the Social Security number on our 1990 taxes wasn't Connie's.

Connie grabbed the credit report, scanned the numbers. The woman has a photographic memory, never wrote down phone numbers. "Look at these Social Security numbers. This's my ex-husband's report, not ours. Don's remarried, also, I never shop designers, ever."

What the hell? I filed joint taxes for 1990 with Connie, our first full year of marriage. Our wedding took place in December 1989. Connie dashed home and pulled the 1989 taxes: married, filed jointly with Don. Oh crap. Somewhere the IRS pulled two numbers out of three. Don's ID and mine appeared on the paperwork. Connie's income and hard-earned credit vanished. Black clouds loomed around her face. Tornado warning.

Instead of paying out the divorce settlement to Don and Chuck, we now had to explain this all to the IRS, that Connie divorced and remarried the same year. Hell, she signed her divorce and we got engaged the same night. Wrote letters. Nothing. Calls to some 800 number, sitting by the phone, none of the robot options a likely choice for this mess. She cussed out the robot on the speaker.

When Connie finally reached a real person I heard, "Oh, you're the one!"

The IRS had listed Don Redifer and Chet Hood as "Married, Filing Jointly." Don and I were now an item.

Oh shit. They obliterated Connie's name, income and credit ratings. Breath steaming into the phone on our end.

"What one?"

"Your letter's on our blooper bulletin board. Two husbands the same year? That's rich. And four people mixed up on one credit rating? You guys have been busy. Anyway, we're resolving your file, and I'll get a letter out. You'll need to get copies into the credit bureaus."

Meanwhile Don and I had papers identifying us as the first same sex marriage in California.

# CHAPTER FORTY-EIGHT

# VANITIES
## WINTER 1993

Oh, how I craved a bubble bath now and then. A deep oversized tub, a vanity, shelves with fluffy towels, English lavender soaps and powders.

Not this morning.

Mornings began with a barefoot run from master bedroom to the tub/shower, squeal of the handle, one more push to the sticky aluminum framed doors and tracks. The track jammed again, but this time the pebbled glass slipped from the frame and crashed, into the floor, the tub, everywhere. The aluminum frame that held the glass came apart.

Stark naked, barefoot in the broken glass. Air turned from pink to blue with screeching commentary about this.

I always hated that 1950s remuddle design in my master bath, painted black plywood cabinets, black and pink formica counters, vinyl wallpaper, all of it. But having it smash into pieces at six in the morning, not good. Dashed downstairs for a quick shower, took off for work. A changed woman walked in the door that evening.

"Chet, let's do the bath! Like grandma's. I'll call John. It's time to do a backwards remodel, a brand new 1910 bath up here."

We knew John from restoration shows, a master craftsman: *expensive*. Restoration focuses on details, learning the craftsmanship of bygone eras, and locating the period pieces you need to finish the project.

Bringing back a luxury bathroom. Maybe a deep tub for bubbles, not a show piece, but a place to relax. Also, a really good shower—big enough for two, massage shower heads for sore shoulders.

Every morning for three years we've stepped around a beveled off corner of the bath, a large mystery space maybe 8 x 8 feet. Not a closet.

Strangely, on Saturdays when I put muffins in the oven, I can go back to bed, smell when they're ready. Jump up, "I think they're done!" and run back downstairs to pull them from the oven. Don't even use a timer. Now why on earth can I smell the kitchen from our upstairs bedroom?

What the hell. We're remodeling anyway. Where's my good hammer? Wham! I crack into the plaster. Layer of concrete underneath. Hit it again, harder. Still mad about the exploding shower this morning. A third blow, and inside the space—nothing.

"Chet, come here! I think we've found the old kitchen chimney!"

John concealed the modern shower inside the old chimney, complete with benches and multiple heads. The awful pink and white wallpaper glued over scored plaster, fake tilework. I order white tile for the walls to go up about five feet. Now to figure out my bathtub. Antique, but long enough for a tall lady.

Our plumber, Gene, retired after more than fifty years in business. Drive to the shop, meet Gene at his darkened front door, gold leaf *"PLUMBING"* mostly scraped off. No more new American Standard fixtures shining in the window. Don't want a modern bathtub anyway. Walk with Gene past pieces of dusty porcelain, old filing cabinets, until we reached the back of his shop. Open another door.

Open rafters of Douglas fir arch over high windows. In this large room lie fixtures he's torn out of houses for fifty years, things that he couldn't bear to part with, a restorer's heaven. "Come on, pick one out. I'd love to give you one of these. Couldn't bear to part with 'em." Claw foot tubs piled along a wall, but one caught the eye, a large deep tub with a simple wrap-around bottom. I'd seen its counterpart "Moderne" in a *Style 1910* magazine.

"You can restore that thing. I'll show you how."

Gene called his crew, loaded the vintage tub on his truck. Got up to the house. The driveway is already stacked with old cabinets, cans of deadly chemicals, and piles of rags and brushes. Everything gets hosed down into the gravel nightly. Be a long time before anything grows in that gravel. Four men lift the cast-iron tub, set it up on sawhorses for me begin the task.

Gene advises, "Get a wire brush and scrape off every bit of loose paint, rust and dirt." On the longer spring days I come home from the office, change into painting clothes, hit the work area and scour. Layers began to look thinner and smoother.

After about the third wire brushing we stripped the tub down to iron. My evil friend, methylchloride, a volatile and toxic chemical solvent. Strips anything. Masks, gloves required. Gene stops by to inspect my work.

"So now do I get to paint it?"

"Oh no. You need to prime it. Needs an undercoat that will help paint stick to metal. Keeps it from rusting."

"You mean, all that crap I just scraped off, don't you? I'm supposed to brush the same stuff on again. "

"Uh huh."

A pedestal sink in beautiful condition turns up at a yard sale in Pasadena. Total cost of my new fixtures? $75.00. Meanwhile, Chet piles brass and copper polish, polishing rags and steel wool into a work bucket. Box after box of nuts and bolts. Eric sits at a worktable with a can of WD-40 and sprays each fixture, then cleans up with a rag. Does it turn? Do you pull it apart? His rags blacken with old grease and dust, a chemical calendar of the twentieth century.

Strained muscles and joints are nothing to us. A few bruises, a scratch here and there. Maybe some strains and sprains. I need to soak, and I want ambience. When you lie in the bathtub, what do you look at? The ceiling of course. A plain white ceiling with a light bulb would not relax anything.

Ooo la la! Why not a French cloudy sky, like the blue ceilings in a chateau, only no saints or cherubs here. I mix blue and green paints, sponge them into the acre of wet Navajo white. Nope. Too dark. Looks like choppy waves. Would make a bather seasick. Tinted and splash on coat after coat—too bright, too dark. Got it pretty much right on the sixth try. That ceiling's stuck together with acrylic paint, won't ever come apart. Then for the motif.

My mom always let me paint cabinets and walls any way I pleased. This time I tackled a new craft, Art Nouveau stencils, collected from house museums. You can't just slap a stencil on the wall. It's important to count out all the bits, center motifs, decide on what's big and what's little. Plan what the corners should look like. Mixed several green paints, first light and sunny, then a second one. Where do the afternoon shadows fall? Deep ocean leaf green there, and with a brush, a few touches of a muddy dark violet. Matches the patterns on the foot of my lady's bathtub, a garden pond.

Last step, pour in the Crabtree and Evelyn, put on music, and dream.

# CHAPTER FORTY-NINE

# LOSING IT
## SPRING 1993

At least the IRS tried to clean up their mess. I had a letter "To Whom it May Concern" that Don and Chet had separated. Their brief marriage over, Don went on to his new life, Chet and I reappeared on clean credit paperwork. Oh, if only escrow were a matter of getting the right money in the right place, on time.

We still had to resolve the plot map with City Hell or our bit of earth wouldn't clear for financing. They had no interest in a lady with a house. Superman left that building years ago. Documents showed that I owned the land outright. Building and Safety inspectors approved and signed off on everything with the house. Over the years two councilmen had been elected and visited the property. Grading Division, the guys who decide whether or not you can build a structure in our earthquake fractured city, refused to sign us off for a Certificate of Occupancy.

My fuse burned away. Don become impatient for his settlement, and the bank didn't understand the hold up on the Certificate of Occupancy. Day after day I went to City Hall with one letter after another notarized, rolls of parcel maps, folders from my city councilwoman.

Maybe a man could get their attention. Chet agreed to go visit Grading Division.

I slipped the hundred-dollar bill into an envelope and told him that the clerk has to see the envelope, or you'll get nothing done. Chet's an actor, but he doesn't lie or cheat. He's been in dozens of films where guys run around shooting, but he'd never confronted guys like these. Their regulations hid inside drawers, stacked on shelves, but they shoved ethical norms into back pockets. Close, but not precisely where they belong.

"What's this?"

Those innocent eyes of his, his straightforward perceptions. Good grief, I'm not asking him to pull off a drug deal.

"I have to send cash, or they won't look at the papers. They file them away and we never hear from them again."

Chet came home, took off his cap, shook his head.

"Did you get the stamp?"

"The clerk looked at the envelope, laid it aside, then, yes, he stamped it. Are you telling me that you've had to drop a C-note on every one of these visits?"

"Pretty much."

"These bastards are taking cash from a frickin' single mother who wants to repair an old house?"

That damn map never cleared. The interim bank couldn't wait any longer. Our loan application had been in process six months, and the balloon payment came due. They would not accept any more monthly payments from me.

"You get your mortgage, or you get a Notice of Default."

"But I can pay this mortgage."

"Your agreement has expired."

I understood much more about hard money. In the default process they would own my property, my investment, and my labor, about $200,000 for a $50,000 loan.

Making the phone call from the office may have a poor choice on my part.

Left my desk, sandwich uneaten, tore out of the parking lot.

Deep breath, to avoid vomiting, strode into Grading Division. Got to the counter. No bribe this time. Just started sobbing. The tough girl broke down, tears and rage. The cubicles quiet, no rustling paper. Everyone at lunch.

"I'm going to lose my home, and it's because of your foul-ups." More tears, tissues, wet tissues crammed in my hands and pockets.

For six years I had been back and forth to City Hall. Once again I stood at the gray Formica counter in Building and Safety, Grading Division, folder in hand. I had no idea how many $100 bills in envelopes I'd handed over, in order to get the pocket protector men to even look at the problem and not bury it in a stack. "Consulting fees" is how my engineer had me note them.

My nose ran, and I really wanted to charge through the gate, screaming, shredding papers, and punching everything in sight. Instead, the tears kept flowing. "I'm going to lose my house. I've done everything you asked, the building inspectors have signed everything, and you people are still looking at the wrong files." Threw the Notice of Default down on the counter.

Planted my feet, pulled out yet another Kleenex. Glared at the desk clerk, who kept averting his eyes. Then he cleared his throat a few times, stepped away.

The desk clerk called to another Senior Inspector, Terry Burgin. Mr. Burgin examined all the papers, including the sign-offs on all my grading permits. Every step we'd carried through, every page correct, on time and on budget, but no Certificate of Occupancy. Burgin checked my red eyes, mascara running. I wiped off my face. He read the Notice of Default from my banker.

"Come with me."

Mr. Burgin opened the gate and led me down rows of cubicles, people burrowed under papers, to a darkened corridor, opened the door to a pink office with windows and artwork on the walls. Behind the immaculate desk sat the Chief of Building and Safety. I handed him my folder. The Chief looked at the packet. He examined my signed permits, the mortgage papers from Security Pacific Bank, and the Notice of Default. The last page inside the folder turned, and the back cover of the file fell into place. He folded his hands and looked across the desk at the inspector and me.

"Why have we held her up like this? Of course, she needs her Certificate of Occupancy." I breathed. A temporary C of O would be ours. I'd pay a $100 fee and we could attack the next set of hurdles. I thanked him. Minutes later the inspector handed me a **Permanent C of O**. I grabbed my checkbook. "Young lady, you've already paid us enough. Enjoy your home."

# CHAPTER FIFTY

# DREAMS WE SEE

The quest? It wasn't ever about owning something. I'm not sure you ever own a house. Shortly after we moved in, over coffee with a friend, I said, "Oh, we don't own that house, that house owns us. We're her stewards."

So, what does this have to do with a garden?

Wildflowers dotted the grasses in the canyon. We love mammoth sunflowers and we had one-third of an acre. Some years sunflowers clustered at the bottom of the lot, delighting everyone who passed through the canyon. One year a friend hoed around the entire perimeter and planted a ten-pound bag of the seeds. Nothing came up. Fat squirrels chattered in our trees, ran along the fence. We laughed at a big boy who tried to jump the posts with an entire avocado in his mouth.

From time to time grasses moved in the canyon. Probably gophers, maybe a coyote. The stables stood vacant, missing their horses from the old days. Ghosts rode out of the shadows, joined us to celebrate glorious afternoons, tipped their hats to legacy and to stewardship.

Our promise to Owl's Nest was that when we were unable to give her the care she needed, we would pass her on to a younger family. For twenty-six years we enjoyed her rooms, our friends, and the gardens. There was laughter and there was tragedy. Eric died of lymphoma at age nineteen. The house folded herself around us like a mother bird. That summer we began digging gardens. One day we got home from church and two trucks were in our driveway. The neighbors had purchased native plants in Eric's memory. Others purchased trees and rocks for us. At the bottom of the hill we installed a theatre.

Several of Eric's college friends were writers, and the theatre became a writer's workshop, a place to run new scripts when they were preparing for submission. We also produced backyard classics, Shakespeare, Shaw and others, often with name actors. Chet directed, I hung out clotheslines of costumes from the trees. People would choose their outfits, step on stage and perform.

We laughed, we mourned, and we told stories. The last play in our theatre was The Tempest. And so Prospero shares his final words.

*We are such stuff*
*As dreams are made on, and our little life*
*Is rounded with a sleep.*

*...*

*Be not disturb'd with my infirmity:*
*If you be pleased, retire into my cell*
*And there repose: a turn or two I'll walk,*
*To still my beating mind.*

# ABOUT THE AUTHOR

Constance Hood retired from teaching with five filing cabinets of family memoirs—tales of war, love, and adventures. Two historical novels emerged from the journals and letters.

*Into Dark Corridors: A Tale of Hands, Heart, and Home* is her own memoir, a tale of falling in love with an old house and keeping promises. Saving the house involved bulldozing a Los Angeles hillside, and moving the large structure in pieces. Then came reassembly, and finally, restoration. The outline for this story originated in two articles written for Craftsman Homeowner Magazine in 1997-1998 *Saving a House from Urban Blight, parts I and II.*

Married to actor Chet Hood, the two spent 26 years working side by side. In 2013 they honored their commitment to the house, that she would live on long after them. The Hoods released stewardship to a new generation and moved to a 1928 home near the beach in Ventura, California.

*Also by Constance Hood:*

*Islands of Deception: Lying with the Enemy*
*Off the Tracks: A Beatnik Family Journey*

For more information, please visit www.Contancehood.com

Made in the USA
Columbia, SC
20 September 2021